To the Little Free Library
Enjoy reading!
With love,
Ann Marie Ruby

ETERNAL TRUTH:

THE TUNNEL OF LIGHT

"Travel with me through the doors of birth, death, reincarnation, true soulmates, dreams, miracles, and end of time, within the eternal truth: the tunnel of light. Throughout time, the unanswered questions have been hidden within the tunnel of light. Through the eyes of a dream psychic, I have walked within this tunnel. With the sacred pen and paper, I walk through my dreams, holding on to the hands of the scientific, religious, and mystical scholars, as I try to answer the unanswered questions of life."

Ann Marie Ruby

Published in the United States of America, 2019.

ISBN-10: 0-578-52937-8

ISBN-13: 978-0-578-52937-0

DEDICATION

From the beginning of time to the present days, we the creation live with the unanswered questions of life. From dawn breaking open with the biggest star smiling upon us till the sighting of the first night star, we wait for all the answers of life. "Ask, seek, and knock," I was told. Yet again, I was told to be happy with what I have, and to not seek the unknown.

Scientists have gone beyond the stars and discovered the universe to be like what was prophesied by religious scholars, mystical philosophers, and seers of the past. To this day, however, scientists can neither disprove nor prove some of the unanswered questions of life. Why? My answer is simple. How can we the creation prove The Creator?

When we are given miracles from the beyond by The Creator, we have a glimpse of the sacred tunnel of light. Just like the scientific and religious scholars, I also believe in miracles. Yet the scholars cannot prove nor disprove them, for miracles are sacred messages from The Creator to the creation. Spread throughout time, these messages have landed upon the sacred souls as we ask, seek, and knock for them. Even though we do not have all the answers, we are happy with the answers our inner mind finds for individual satisfaction. I believe the biggest miracles are hidden within the questions, as for these unanswered questions, we the creation keep moving toward the miraculous tunnel of light. This tunnel hides within its soul all the blessed secrets of life.

I have walked in this tunnel through my sacred dreams, scientific facts, and religious facts to bring to you my answers to the unanswered questions of life. This tunnel has been visited by children and adults, as documented throughout time. All the visitors of this sacred tunnel are blessed as they are our only witnesses to this miraculous tunnel. I believe this tunnel is The Creator's blessing to all of the creation.

After my personal journey through various miracles of life, I dedicate this book to the tunnel, known to scientists as the Near-Death Experience (NDE) tunnel, and to others as the miraculous tunnel of light.

TABLE OF CONTENTS

MESSAGE FROM THE AUTHOR

"Messages are left as ashes, buried within Earth, throughout time. Yet, from the door of miracles, they ask, seek, and knock for our attention as they find their seekers."

As a dream psychic, I walk in life through the views of the past, present, and future. What lies ahead is not known, yet messages are found through the door of miracles, within the miraculous tunnel of light. Do we always follow these sacred messages, or do we ignore them? I have done both.

I learned to accept the messages with caution of the human mind. Humans are generally cautious as the mind warns us to decide for ourselves. Sometimes, our decisions are on target, but at other times, we live with regret and learn to walk ahead. This book is here for you to take some time and look within your inner soul. What is faith to you? Is your mind always searching for something more? The answers are not known to us the humans, but we know they are out there.

We the humans have traveled across the oceans and above the skies, to the moon and beyond. Why do we still not have the answers to our asked and unasked questions? I am a seeker who asks, seeks, and knocks upon the door of miracles for the answers. After the sun sets, we are left within the dark night, where we need guidance from the beyond.

I believe the stars above and the Earth beneath our feet have all the secrets buried within them. We the humans have taken birth upon this Earth and we take our final resting place upon her chest. Yet, we leave behind the unknown answers as we finish our journey through this life. Today, I want you to walk with me through the eyes of a dream psychic as we travel from the past, through the present, to the future. With only my eyes, I will walk through the views of the past seers, religious scholars, and scientific scholars.

For my own self, I had noted down my journey through my personal findings. Today, I write my personal thoughts for you. I have walked through the tunnel of light. Now I want all of you to walk through my journal and write your own stories as you too join this quest to find the *Eternal Truth: The Tunnel Of Light*.

INTRODUCTION

"Introduced to life we are at birth, as Mother Earth welcomes us. With a loud cry, we enter. Our journey ends, accompanied by salty tears, as we the children are returned to Mother Earth. Each soul, however, leaves behind sacred answers for the future generation through the individual life lived."

Within the pages of religious scholars, we travel through the mythological and Abrahamic periods. Throughout time, religious scholars have tried to guide us through the doors of miracles and dreams. Many of us agreed with the scholars and followed them periodically, yet we differed from land to land.

Time changes the personal perspectives of the perceivers as with time, messages change from mouth to mouth. The sources differ, but one topic that remains the same is the tunnel of light. With all miracles, we always have the powerful glow of light.

The scientific scholars have included themselves within this search and have tried to answer our unanswered questions. Why are there so many differences within the opinions of the scholars? Differences in opinions have created divisions amongst the humans as humans have created different religions and groups. To this day, we the humans follow various religions. Some of us are just spiritual without any religious belief.

Today, there is a spike in the number of people who believe religion is the cause of division. After knocking upon all different doors, these humans have decided they believe in a superior power, but follow no religion. We the humans, however, believe in birth, death, and dreams. Even scientific scholars believe in these aspects that have been proven throughout time. In addition to these three topics, I personally believe in reincarnation, twin flames, and miracles. I know as everything ends, it is then the end of time.

Whenever we the creation come upon a closed door, we knock upon the door of miracles. Our quest has led the religious and scientific scholars to their own discoveries and answers. All have come upon the tunnel of light through their research and seeking. The miraculous staircase to Heaven, or the tunnel of light, brought me to the scientific scholars and their research papers about the NDE tunnel. I believe the tunnel of light is the same as the NDE tunnel.

I share my perspective through the guidance of miracles, and with the help of the scientific, religious, and mystical scholars. Miracles from the beyond are just that miracles, yet sometimes we are shown the evidence of these miracles. Life is a miracle from birth till death. Whatever begins must also end, as this is the truth The Lord, The Creator has bestowed upon us. Walk with me as we explore the unanswered questions of life through my eyes, within the *Eternal Truth: The Tunnel of Light*.

CHAPTER ONE

BIRTH:
THE TUNNEL OF ENTRY

"Through the tunnel of light, enter all the living, thus begins the journey through life."

-Ann Marie Ruby

Washington State is my hometown where my log cottage sits within the warmth of her stone fireplace. I watch Mount Rainier standing tall amongst us, reminding us how beautiful she is. Snow-covered mountains have elk and deer roaming around in peace and harmony.

Today, I watched two geese sitting within my pond waiting for their babies to be born. Two ducks have also taken shelter within the pond. Nature is perfect as within this, I find my inner peace and comfort. Through the tunnel of light, dawn brought to my soul the blessed birth of a new day.

Nature pulls me toward her as I find all my inspiration within this Earth and beyond. Dawn and dusk are the blessed free gifts our Creator has bestowed upon us. As a child, I had asked my Lord to never take these blessed gifts away from me. I would cry in fear thinking what if dawn never came and left me within the dark.

I had walked with my father as he told me to always remember the blinking stars up above in the night sky are there for us as guides. His words remain in my soul even today when I search for him within the night sky. I wonder which star he is. Why did he have to join the night stars? I know he had answered me when I was a child.

He had said one day, he too would go up there to guide all of the lost and stranded souls. Even to this day when I see a tornado, I have a strange feeling. I wonder if like a tornado, a tunnel had appeared to take my father high up to the house in Heaven. We are all blessed as throughout the days and throughout the nights, we have the sun and the moon guiding all the lost and stranded souls. The stars are our angels in disguise. I know we have humans walking around who are also our guiding angels.

My hidden fears were the unasked questions of my inner soul which I had wanted to ask my father, yet I knew these questions were not to be asked. I wanted to ask the preachers within my church, but the fear of being criticized prevented me from asking these questions. Humans are born and shall die as life is The Creator's gift to all of us. The questions still remain. Where do we the humans come from? My question is not how we are born, but where we come from. How do we enter Earth as we are born? Why are there so many religions as we are all the creation of The One Creator?

I never asked my father or anyone else these questions as I knew the answers differed from human to human. Parallel answers came from different religions and different beliefs, but the answers still remain unknown. What is birth? What could Mother Earth teach us about the birth of humans? Is she not the only witness who has seen it all firsthand?

The sun is around 4.6 billion years old. The sun and the solar system took birth within a cloud of gas, or solar nebula. This nebular theory is accepted by a lot of scientists; however, not all scientists agree. The Roman name Nebula translates to clouds, also known as Nephele, a mythological Greek goddess who was raped and as a result, gave birth to centaurs. Mythological stories differ as there are so many stories and versions.

I always wondered why mythological and Biblical stories were so alike, but different from mouth to mouth. If we move from mythology to the Abrahamic religions, we also find stories about creation, rape, childbirth, jealousy, and brother going against brother. Some Biblical scholars believe Eve was raped while others reject this belief. We will never know what really happened within the mythological and Biblical stories as we do not have the full stories.

In Abrahamic religions, the first known birth and sin began as humans entered Earth. Upon Earth, there are stories of Adam and Eve, murder, and the first death linked to their sons Cain and Abel. In the journey through life, we do not know what we are destined to because we create our own destiny. What we do know is we all entered Earth and started to live within and amongst sin.

Adam and Eve are known as the father and mother figures of us the humans. My question again is how did we end up on Earth? If all came from The One Creator, and from the original parents, then why have so many different religions taken birth, claiming to be the only path back to The Creator?

My mind had the unanswered questions as I was neither looking for how the Earth was created, nor who the first creation on Earth was, but how we the creation came upon Earth. We know all creation exist, but the question for me was how? Did we travel somehow? Are we just born without any source? But then, how did the first source end up on Earth?

Scientific evidence has shadowed a lot of religious beliefs. I always look at the scientific and religious views when forming my personal view. I know life is a blessing and all humans have interconnecting relationships with one another. The stories from different religions and the scientific answers for them could not satisfy my unanswered questions about how we came upon this Earth.

I learn about the truth as taught within each individual religion and not disproven by science. As a spiritually awakened person, I know we the humans have a direct connection with our Creator beyond human understanding. Throughout time, religious scholars and scientific scholars have agreed upon one path, miracles do exist that are above human comprehension. Birth of all existence, including us the humans, has come from the unknown to begin our journey through life.

The questions remain. How are we upon this Earth? Where have we come from, and why? The War in Heaven was discussed in the Bible and other religious books, but why had this war begun? Religious scholars have tried to answer these questions through different perspectives, for the personal minds. Like the religious scholars, I too search for the answers. I believe some things are not for us the humans to know for we may not be able to handle the knowledge.

We must find peace within our chosen paths, guided by our basic moral values. When and where we have a direct connection to the divine light, it is then and there we find peace, or I must say peace finds us. I had started to meditate as the obstacles of life had knocked upon my door. I allowed peace to knock upon my door through the positive vibes found throughout this universe.

I had dreams about running away from danger in what I knew was the War in Heaven. After a lot of dreams, I researched and found out something had happened in Heaven. Maybe some of us remember and some do not. For you today, I have a different kind of dream. All mythological and Abrahamic religions agree we were sent to Earth for a reason. People from different faiths have witnessed a war and running from Heaven in their dreams. We know something must have happened and we were sent to Earth for a reason. I am assuming we were sent here for a test, but how? I had a dream within which I had received some answers.

My dream:

There was light. It was so peaceful,
yet I knew there was a rush. I was running

through a tunnel. I knew this tunnel so well as if I had traveled through this tunnel before. I watched so many people running in all different directions.

I saw the tunnel looked like a big glowing light where there were doors in all directions. Each door had something written on it and I knew I must find the end of the tunnel. I watched upon the doors were blinking lights where one was labeled birth, and another one was labeled death.

I had wanted to walk through a specific door that was labeled God The Creator. That is when I heard a voice say, "Not yet. It is not time yet." I saw a man running as I wanted to see what was happening. I saw The Holy Archangels hold on to my hands as they said, "Watch."

I watched a few people run in a direction and as they were running, they were becoming younger and younger. An elderly man looked like a teenager as he ran toward the end of the tunnel. I watched this same person then became a child and took the form of a bird. The bird looked like he was made out of light. I saw the bird fly and enter Earth into the womb of his Earthly mother.

The Earthly mother was about to give birth to her Earthly son. As I watched, I wondered was the soul entering the body at the final stage? Or is it when the body is being released from the mother's womb, another tunnel, is when the lightning bolt, the bird, or the soul unites with his or her physical body? I heard the cries of a young baby and the joy and laughter of the parents upon receiving their child.

From different directions, humans were jumping onto Earth like bolts of lightning. The tunnel began from a huge dark room. Someone had held on to my hands as I said, "Archangel Gabriel." He smiled and said, "Walk with us and just observe."

I was with The Holy Archangels and remember running to the end of the tunnel. The Holy Archangels said, "This is the tunnel of birth everyone must enter through to go upon Earth." I asked, "What had happened within Heaven that all humans had to jump onto Earth?" They smiled, kissed my head, and said, "Watch." I had watched this dream just as a witness and knew I must remember this dream.

My dream had broken as I watched dawn approach through the night sky. We the humans forget our travel journey from Heaven to Earth, but somehow, some of us walk with memories of the War in Heaven and running away from it. Some awaken with the feeling of being lost, wondering what we are here for. According to the religious scholars, we are all here for a test, or to prove we can avoid sin and become the pure and the pious.

NDE is a term which scientists use to explain near-death experiences. Witnesses of NDEs have testified walking through a tunnel, which was made out of light. From these experiences, the name came to be known as the tunnel of light, or the tunnel of life. NDEs have brought this knowledge upon us as a gift from the beyond. I feel we use this same tunnel when we enter this Earth and take birth. Is it not true if you have an entry way, then you must have an exit too?

In my dream, as I was walking through the tunnel of light, I wondered why there were so many different doors. I wanted so much to walk through one door where my Lord, my Creator was. I assumed we travel through the door labeled birth to take birth upon Earth. As we enter, many believe, the soul chooses his or her parents.

We exit through the door of death at the end of our life. I always believe and keep within my faith, life on this Earth is but a day as the consort of life is death. After death, we take the same tunnel and then travel through the door of either the pious or the sinners.

I had seen The Holy Archangels watching over all as we the humans had begun our journey. Within this journey, we must learn to travel alone within the commandments of The Lord, The Creator. I felt like there was a judgment within Heaven for which we were born within our humanly status. Maybe we are all here trying to repent, redeem, and awaken in death, sin free, pure, and clean because of our committed sins in Heaven. Asleep we are within life. I believe we are awakened in death rather than in life, as within death our knowledge is given back to us.

It is within life, we must travel with complete faith, and not break the rules for we are the travelers. I know people have questioned why we should follow the laws of The Lord, The God who is unknown to all. My answer is simple. Follow the laws of your land and honor the people around you. It is then, you have also followed the laws of The Lord, The Creator.

In other dreams, I knew with me, I had seen my soulmate and our children running too. Other women and men I knew were also running through the birth tunnel. I wondered is that why we were all born with families and friends? Do we get lost from each other as we come closer to Earth? I do not know what had happened to us or all the people who had run with us. All the humans were being born on Earth as children without any memories.

The answers to my questions remained unknown as we had entered the tunnel of light to arrive on Earth. We the humans choose our path as per our will and our way. We choose our birth and our life our own way, but death chooses us his own way. The soul has the freedom to live life according to his or her own will. Religious scholars agree the soul is immortal. According to research by Dr. Jim B. Tucker, a scientist at the University of Virginia,

> "One out of five children who report a past life say they recall the intermission, the time between death and birth, although there is no consistent view of what that's like. Some allege they were in 'God's house,' while others claim they waited near where they died before 'going inside' their mother" (Lyons).

Scientists know life is a reality just like death is a fact. They have proven that we do see dreams. Yet, no one knows the hidden miracles behind these proven facts. Scientists have traveled to the cosmos to find what lies past the reality of the known. Advanced scientific research shows us the pictures of the cosmos beyond what the normal eyes can see.

Throughout time, the seers have left for us their drawn versions of the cosmos and the future seen through their visions from the past, such as Michel de Nostredame, also known as Nostradamus. What do I see as a seer? Birth is a miracle as we enter the tunnel of light, as is death. Death is not the end of life but the beginning of a journey through the same tunnel of light. This tunnel, known to all as the time tunnel, does exist. Through birth and death, we are able to be there. Within us, there are some who can travel through this tunnel through the doors of dreams and miracles.

One scientist who is said to have traveled through the door of dreams and give birth to a wonderful gift for the world is Dmitri Mendeleev. All matter whether in the cosmos or on Earth is created with atoms and chemical elements, some we know of and some we may not know of yet. Children learn about these chemical elements using the periodic table. Although many scientists have contributed to it, Dmitri Mendeleev is often referred to as the father of the periodic table we use today.

When Dmitri Mendeleev's mother was passing away, "Her last words to her favourite son were typically forceful: 'Refrain from illusions, insist on work and not on words. Patiently seek divine and scientific truth'" (Strathern 264-265). While seeking a way to organize the elements, Dmitri Mendeleev is believed to have said, "In a dream I saw a table where all the elements fell into place as required.

Awakening, I immediately wrote it down on a piece of paper" ("Dmitri Mendeleev").

The year 2019 marks the 150th birthday of the periodic table. The United Nations General Assembly proclaimed and UNESCO approved 2019 to be the International Year of the Periodic Table of Chemical Elements. They see the periodic table "as one of the most important and influential achievements in modern science reflecting the essence not only of chemistry, but also of physics, biology and other basic sciences disciplines" ("Official launch").

The periodic table had celebrated its 150th birthday, and it shall celebrate many more beyond our time. This miracle birth had taken place within the tunnel of light as it was accepted by its father through his blessed dream. Whether you choose to accept his dream, or you reject it as just a story told and retold throughout time, the periodic table is used by scientists and students worldwide even to this day to study the chemical elements.

My point is miracles are just that, miracles. Some of us follow the miracles through our religious beliefs. Others only accept the scientifically proven theories. Do remember the past seers had predicted the future through their visions which are only proven to be true through the tunnel of time to the future.

It may sound scary, but within the same tunnel, all life must travel. Upon our hands, we have the deeds of our life to take us to yet another blessed place where miracles begin again. For evidence of my theory, I take you to the NDE theory as this proves the tunnel. No scientist can completely disprove or explain the reasoning behind this tunnel, for how can you know the truth of the beyond unless you have come back from death yourself?

No thoughts or proofs can explain why and how we the humans have ended upon Earth. Believe in yourself and know all of this is a complete miracle. If life could be explained scientifically, then how would science explain the dead communicating with the living?

From the other side, our beloved ones guide us, and at times, they haunt us. Why and how? I believe life is a miracle where all of us must enter this tunnel of light. What happens if we get lost within this tunnel, just like we get lost within the highways of life? The lost and stranded souls must find peace through their personal beliefs and ways of life.

When you the traveler have the address, you shall end up at the right door, The Door of The Omnipotent. What if you do not know who your Creator is, and you are knocking on the wrong door? What happens then? Is it then we are the lost and stranded? I know this is the question that has divided all humans into different groups and faiths.

My advice is to follow the laws of the land and be good to all. If your religion asks you to do something that goes against the basic moral values, then it is wrong. You the individual traveler shall know the truth. Your inner guiding light shall guide you to the truth.

Here, I have a prayer for you from my prayer book, *Spiritual Songs II: Blessings From A Sacred Soul.*

BELOVED CREATOR, THE ALPHA, THE OMEGA

Life blesses all at birth.
Life glows within all throughout eternity,
For I know my Lord, this life was created
Before my entry onto Earth.
This life was, is, and shall always be blessed,
As it is but the complete blessing of

My Lord, my Creator.

Blessed is but the birth of all souls as the soul is

But always complete within the complete love

And devotion of The Creator.

My Lord, my Creator but loves this creation

For I was but created by my

BELOVED CREATOR,

THE ALPHA,

THE OMEGA.

The spiritual enlightenment awakens all of the inner mind, body, and soul to the complete understanding between The Creator and the creation. When the direct connection is created, it is then the immense love for The Creator enlightens the inner faith and all the answers are found. With birth through the tunnel of light, we the creation had begun our blessed journey. Aside from religion, the scientific community has proven this tunnel through the blessed eyes of us the creation. Our Creator with so much love has given these sightings as answers for our sought questions.

Remember you had taken the journey to this Earth alone as you entered the tunnel of light. Do I believe in the birth tunnel, through which we the humans enter? I do. We are here. We enter this world and exit this world after our journey through life. Our soul lives on even after our physical death on Earth. Aside from religion, science too could not disprove the traveling journey of the soul before birth or after death.

Science came up with the term NDE to describe part of this journey. Scientists have gathered evidence of people's experiences through this tunnel. I believe as my dreams, science, religion, and all the living proof testify, birth is but the entry, and death is but the exit. Religious houses are homes which guide all humans like a lighthouse to live upon this Earth with dignity, honor, and courage.

Science has proven a lot of asked questions of inquiring minds. Like Dmitri Mendeleev and the periodic table, some scientific theories have come to us through the scientific scholars and their dreams. Here I know like them, I too saw my proofs within dreams.

The entry and exit are but through the same tunnel of light, as we all return to The One Creator. So, let us not divide amongst each other. Let us accept the differences and live with each other, for each other, as we are all travelers through life. Life is a miracle which ends as she finally meets her consort which is known to all as death.

CHAPTER TWO

DEATH:
THE TUNNEL OF EXIT

"The day begins and ends as life on this Earth is but a day."

-Ann Marie Ruby

"The mountain is out" is a phrase known to all residing within the foothills of Mount Rainer. It means the day is clear and we all have a perfect view of the mountain. The snow-covered mountain view is the backdrop of so many picture-perfect memories. Today, I had the shivers, thinking she is active, yet asleep. What if she wakes up and erupts again? She is one of the most dangerous volcanoes on this Earth. As I held on to my shawl to take cover from the chilly spring morning, I thought about death and how it is not an end but the beginning to yet another chapter.

Through the tunnel of light, birth and death of all creation and all existence are found within this Earth. Throughout time, different mythologies have taught the sun was carried away and brought back to us by powerful horses. Now, advanced science has taught us about our solar system. Dawn comes upon our door as the sun appears through the dark night skies. At dusk, however, the sun disappears. As we bid our farewell, we know we shall unite again at dawn.

The universe is a sample of life as within the Earth and beyond, we find examples of the cosmos within our individual lives. The sun gives light to different parts of the world at different times every day. So many stories were told throughout time as to what happens until we realized through scientific revelations, the complete truth.

What about the human who leaves us as Earthly death comes to the human body? Is it then the body becomes invisible, but the soul remains alive throughout time? Just like the sun never leaves and we just move forward, do the dead remain in the past, when we the future move on through the time tunnel? I had always wondered if I could go back in time, would I find the deceased still living life as we had left them behind?

The scientific term of death is known as the irreversible loss of all circulatory and respiratory functions. It is then the life lived becomes just a memory. Religions have their own perspectives on death. A life lost in all religions is but lost.

Here, we all agree. It is strange how divided we the humans are within our perspectives on life, death, birth, and the reason for being on Earth. Despite the divisions within our perspectives, death cannot be prevented as birth is also agreed upon.

Some people have had NDEs. The specific term NDE was developed by Dr. Raymond Moody in the 1970s to describe near-death experiences, although knowledge of the tunnel existed from before. He had interviewed thousands of patients who had witnessed a tunnel of light.

All of them had come close to death. Some were pronounced dead, but came back to life. During NDEs, people see their own bodies lying on the hospital bed, and they see a tunnel. These people had tried to return to their bodies. We now have the NDE theory because they had returned and were able to talk about their experiences.

Death is a destiny all the living shall knock upon. Within the United States, over 2.6 million people die each year. Death within all religions is known as the ending for all that had begun.

Some believe in resurrection after death. Some believe in reincarnation, and some believe in nothingness. Christianity and Islam believe in the afterlife of the soul. Hinduism, Sikhism, Jainism, Buddhism, and others believe in reincarnation.

The judgment day, the bad deeds, and the good deeds are also beliefs of different religions. I know and believe in the tunnel of light as aside from the religious scholars, even science cannot disprove the tunnel through which the soul enters and exits. So, what happens after death? How do the dead communicate with the living if all had ended at death?

Death is inevitable and all the travelers must come upon this path. How do I know about the tunnel of light aside from my dreams? Scientific scholars testify through their research of patients with NDEs, what I too have personally witnessed. I had a very small outpatient procedure done. It was not something I needed to do, but I had wanted to do this. As I had trusted my doctor, I walked into this nightmare which had my faith in doctors leave my soul for a while.

When I awakened after the procedure, I had told the doctors, the biggest surgery for me was my gall bladder surgery. The doctors, however, were very upset as I asked them if something was wrong. They had told me I was dying, and I had internal bleeding because one of the doctors had accidently cut something. They had taken me back to surgery and I had a dream during my surgery.

My dream:

> I saw I was walking through a tunnel
> and my Lord was there waiting for me. I ran
> toward Him as I started to cry and told Him
> how all of my life, I had waited for Him. I

told Him how I had always tried to avoid sin, for I loved my Lord, my Creator.

My Lord told me to wait and rethink if I wanted to continue or go back. I asked, "But why?" He told me, "Watch."

I saw behind me, my mother had been crying and I felt terrible for her. I watched the doctors trying to bring me back. I saw them asking each other, "What could have happened? She was completely healthy! What is going on?"

The whole thing was strange as I could see everyone and hear everyone, but they could not see or hear me. I also saw my physical body and it was very strange as I did not have any feelings for my physical body. I thought I was complete and did not relate my soul to my physical body.

I do not know what the dead feel, but if this is how they feel, then they are in peace. I was worried about my mother, father, and other family members, none of whom had been there, as the procedure was not even something anyone worried about.

I saw in front of me I had my future which was hard, but a life left to live. I told my Lord I will be back after I finish the unfinished jobs left to be completed by me. The tunnel was revolving, and it was made out of light. I knew in front of me was my home. I wanted to walk forward and continue, but I knew my work on Earth was not yet completed.

When I awakened, I asked the nurse in charge if I had just died. She said the doctors had brought me back, and I am amongst the living. I did not really feel good listening to the nurse's remarks, but I was in no condition to say anything. She had said my father had called as he had a dream I was dying. My sister also had a dream in which she had gone to a psychic, who had told her I had died.

My sister and father had called to find out I almost did die, and I had no one with me. I had told all I am never alone as I always have my Lord, my Creator with me at all times. Life is a miracle where sometimes you have family all around you, and at times you have no one. Other people become your family as they welcome you and you welcome them as soul families.

Dr. Sam Parnia has done extensive research, and continues to seek scientific evidence of what happens during NDEs, specifically the experiences of cardiac arrest survivors. "Research into 'near-death' experiences has revealed that awareness and the mind may continue to exist after the brain has ceased to function and the body is clinically dead" (Smith and Steere). According to Dr. Sam Parnia, "The evidence thus far suggests that in the first few minutes after death, consciousness is not annihilated" (Smith and Steere).

As the medical team was trying to bring me back, even though my physical body was not moving, I was conscious of everything that was happening inside the room. My personal experience stayed with me for years. I found out firsthand that the tunnel of light as so many call it, is not a myth but a fact. NDE is a reality proven not only through various religions, but through science too.

My quest is not how we die or why, but what happens after death. I have received messages from deceased people within my dreams. I share one particular dream as I had never met or known the deceased person.

My dream:

> I saw a woman who was unknown to me. Her car was deep in the water and she kept asking me to help her as she was dying. I saw her car had slipped off of the curb and fell into a ditch. She could not get out and now was drowning in very shallow water as the car door had jammed. I tried to do something to help her, but I felt I was watching like a spirit, as I had held on to the hands of The Holy Archangels.

> The strangest part of the dream was she told me her employer did not have her mother's address, so her employer would not know of her living relatives. She begged if her body could be returned to her mother. She saw me as I could see her, but I could not help her.

> I watched her walk into the tunnel of light. As she walked within it, she found a

door where she could call for help. I knew of the tunnel she had entered. I knew if she had any last wishes left on Earth, she would be lost in this tunnel until her wishes were granted.

I saw Angels standing there as they told me it is always the lost who try to communicate with someone who can hear them for their last wishes. I knew I had seen my relatives walking within this tunnel of light. They had kissed me their farewell until we meet again. Yet this was a complete stranger who told me her name.

I had tried to communicate with her as I watched her looking down at her body. I knew she was free from all the pain and feelings left on Earth, but she kept looking at her body. I did not know what connection the soul had with the body, but I knew somehow her physical body needed to be returned to her family.

My dream broke and I started to cry as I did not know who she was. I jumped up and immediately called my friends. I mentioned the woman's name and asked if they knew of her. One of them got the chills as he said his company did have a short-term employee by that name. He called his work and heard his employer repeat the same story.

A short-term employee had died on a tour within a foreign country. The group had just landed, and her car slipped off of the curb. Everyone was saved but one person as her car door had jammed. Her employer did not have any records of her relatives as she was not in touch with her family after a break up. After my insistence, her employer discovered she did have a mother with whom she had no contact for years. Her brother had come to take her back home.

This was a strange knock as I have written about other incidents when I had received calls from the beyond asking for help. I have been blessed, but you could say at times it feels like a burden. When and where I can help, it feels good, but when I cannot do anything, it feels like I have let myself and others down. On another occasion, I had another dream.

My dream:

> I saw my aunt had passed away. My family members did not inform me of her passing. I had a visit from her as she appeared with a great burden and loss of words.

> She was terrified as she was buried at a place far away from her family and friends. She cried and told me that she was buried in a new city and town where she did not know anyone. She asked why they would do this even after they all knew of her last wish.

> I hugged her and asked her to find peace within herself and be the forgiving one even if they had not respected her last wish. I told her not to let this be a burden for she must move on and find peace as she walks through the tunnel. Her body was where it was and she must let her soul be in peace with the knowledge that she is now within the house of The Lord, The Creator.

> She smiled and promised she would find peace in forgiving. She hugged me and

moved on. My dream broke as dawn had peeked through the night skies.

I called my family and asked them if everything was okay or if there was any news. They told me at that time, my aunt had passed away peacefully and was buried in peace. I asked where she was buried and found out they had buried her near their home. I asked if she wanted to be buried there or if she had asked to be buried at any specific place.

I was told yes, her dying wish was to be buried near her family members, but it was not possible financially or physically. They had done this as they had no other choice. Her other family members who lived where she wanted to be buried did not help either. I had shared my dream with them.

At times, it is hard to explain my personal feelings. I did not know why I had seen this dream because I barely knew this aunt. I tried to convey my messages, but what do I do when her burial was already complete? I prayed for her to find peace within her soul and may we the living try to at least respect the last wishes, as even when they are gone, they live on.

My dreams prove that yes even after death, there are different doors through which people still have emotional connections to this Earth. All must enter the tunnel of light and walk through the door of death, yet some get lost. I believe this is how we have evil spirits roaming around. We must try to complete the individual's last wishes. If we are unable to do so for any reason, we must seek forgiveness for them and ask them to forgive us.

I wondered why God would allow evil to roam around freely. I guess that is where free will comes in. People who are evil in life still remain evil in death. Why would they change after death? I believe in the final judgment as it is then we shall be judged. I have seen the Egyptian mummies were buried with their Earthly belongings as they too believed in the afterlife. In modern days, it is hard for me to sometimes remember all of the miracles life but leaves behind for us.

The founding father of the Netherlands, William the Silent, was born on April 24, 1533 in the House of Nassau. In addition to being Count of Nassau-Dillenburg, in 1544, he received the title Prince of Orange. William the Silent is the ancestor of the current monarchy of the Netherlands.

He was a man who had been very close to God. As the Protestants were being persecuted for their religious beliefs, he had objected. This had struck the humanity within him. Even though he was born as a Lutheran, he had the upbringing and education of a Roman Catholic.

Within the New Church in Delft is but laid to sleep the founder of this blessed nation. During my visit to the New Church, I was told that William the Silent had requested to have the two top buttons of his shirt unbuttoned when he passed away, so his soul could go in peace. As William the Silent lay dying, he had said, "My God, have mercy on my soul and on these poor people." This is one of the versions of his last words as they vary slightly due to translation, but the message remains the same.

All the monarchs of the Netherlands are laid within the New Church in Delft, where their founding father was laid to rest. All the Dutch kings, queens, their consorts, and children can choose whether to be embalmed or not as they eventually go into their resting place within this church. On the crypt of the founding father of the Netherlands, it says, "Here lies William I, Father of the Fatherland, awaiting the resurrection."

What an amazing family he has with honorable family members who have accepted death as a blessing. They have taught me even without their own realization, death is not to be feared, for it is the only destination that is guaranteed. My visit to this historical place had intensified faith within my soul. If life is a celebration through gaining knowledge, then death is the final graduation.

Waiting for resurrection, or within some religions, reincarnation, or just the judgment days, we are all destined to the door of death. The life lived is eternal through the memories left behind. If time is frozen, then maybe all life would be frozen in time.

On the Day of Judgment, will we all see each other as the magical door of time that separates us disappears? Miracles are just that, miracles. Until the miracle happens, we wait for it to arrive at our doors.

Throughout time, people have said that religions came into existence because of the fear of death. I believe it is not the fear of death, but the need to find out what happens to the dead is what created different religions. The seekers sought religion, wishing to know what happened to their loved ones, and where they are. Our inner soul's love and longing but seek the answers.

Complete faith I have in life and within the afterlife. Dreams are a reality and today even science has proven the facts of dreams. The content of dreams no one knows, but you the individual. This individual believes we will reunite with our loved ones as they have all taken shelter within the house of The Omnipotent.

Their tests have ended and as they await the results, we are still travelers within this journey of life. We have as support, the guidance of the past travelers and the love for the future travelers as we do our share of the journey. Leave behind hope and blessings as we light candles for the past and become the candles of hope for the future.

Life is a journey from our entry to our exit, through the tunnel of light. Here, we the humans kiss life and embrace her journey with a welcome hug. Remember to not forget even after our journey ends upon this Earth, our journey continues through the tunnel of light to yet another beginning. At this section, hold on to the hands of the blessed Angels who are guiding us throughout eternity.

For all of you, here I have a prayer from my book, *Spiritual Songs: Letters From My Chest.*

DEATH KISSES GENTLY
FOR DEATH IS KIND

Death kisses gently for death is kind.

Death comes over within our lifetime.

Oh my Lord.

Oh my Lord.

Oh my Lord,

My entire life just passed by within a blink.

Time waits not at my door as death stops by.

My Lord, I smell the wonderful breeze of death

As my windows and doors open welcoming him.

Oh my Lord,

May my soul fly over within the peaceful wind,

When it is my time.

May I be gentle.

May I be kind.

May I be brave when the wind blows the chimes

To announce my time.

My Lord forgive me.

My Lord forgive me.

My Lord forgive me,

For I carry the burden of my sins.

My sinful body is ashamed and heavy

For the flight.

My sinful body is a burden for my soul.

My heart, filled with eternal grief, howls

For my Lord.

My Lord, may my body be sin free.

My Lord, may my soul be free

From all Earthly sins.

My Lord, may I be forgiven before my last breath.

My Lord, may I cross the bridge

Within Your arms, within Your guidance,

Blessed amidst Your love.

May I be amongst Your true devotees my Lord,

For I know as the day ends,

Dark nights will take over.

My Lord, amidst all the darkness,

May Your tunnel of light guide me.

My Lord, I place my hands together

For my last prayer,

Take me Home to The House of my Lord.

My Lord, when The Merciful Angel of Death

Reaches my door for I know then it is my time,

I pray to You, my Lord,

DEATH KISSES GENTLY
FOR DEATH IS KIND.

Touched by the blessed kiss of an Angel, we enter the door of death, through the tunnel of exit. Do not fear death as death is a new beginning, an adventure where we too can guide the future travelers. Teachers of life we all become as we travel for love, teaching all to unite through life and death. How do we leave this Earth? What happens after death? Can the dead communicate with us?

Life is a journey for all of us the travelers. We enter this world knowing this is our temporary home. We must return to where we had come from, proving both our birth and death are confirmed. The physical body is discarded, yet our soul travels through the tunnel which scientists have described through NDEs.

Through the blessed humans, we were invited to their individual visions. We had landed upon the NDEs and the blessed hands of the doctors whom hold on to the hands of all of these humans. Through religion and now various scientific researches, this tunnel has been proven.

I know through the door of dreams, the dead do communicate with the living. People have used

Electromagnetic Field (EMF) detectors to prove these paranormal experiences do happen. We have seen some souls do not travel home, but they stay back.

Do I believe in death and the final journey? I do. I believe in the NDE tunnels, and that through dreams and other sources, the dead do communicate with the living. Remember always, never fear death for in death, there should be no fears or tears, but only joy of moving on. When one moves on, hope lives on through faith. Within faith, we know where there is death, some religions believe in resurrection and some believe in reincarnation.

CHAPTER THREE

REINCARNATION: THE CYCLE OF LIFE

"As the soul travels to rejuvenate and awakens within a new vehicle, with or without memories, we begin again."

-Ann Marie Ruby

Morning dew and morning glories are my blessed friends during my morning walk. Deep breathing and relaxing within nature are my first welcome prayers of the day. I know the fish in my pond welcome their morning feed as they all come up to their breakfast whenever they hear my voice.

Today, I watched a crane sitting at the dock waiting for the fish. I saw she had something in her mouth as she flew away. I cried for the fish yet remembered what my friend had told me a long time ago. Life is a circle, so believe in reincarnation as the first blessing of dawn.

Dawn marks the birth of a day and dusk marks its end, or death. With the birth of a new day, my mind dwells within the thoughts of reincarnation. The personal journey of a traveler's soul continues through the tunnel of light until the soul transmigrates into a new physical body, after the death of the current body.

The journey then continues with a newly found vehicle where life ends yet begins again. Through the tunnel of light as we travel, I have seen within my dreams there are different doors, with different names upon them. One of the doors is called the door of reincarnation.

This is a journey millions of people believe in, as they believe in reincarnation. Reincarnation has evolved from mythology to science. Mainly a concept in Hinduism, Buddhism, Jainism, Sikhism, and mysticism, reincarnation is a theory some scientists believe in, yet some disregard it as just a personal belief. Some scientists also disregard religion completely and regard religion as an individual belief system.

Dr. Ian Stevenson, former professor of psychiatry at the University of Virginia, had dedicated most of his life to this research. He had researched to prove reincarnation as a fact. According to Dr. Ian Stevenson, "[T]he most promising evidence bearing on reincarnation seems to come from the spontaneous cases, especially among children" (3). People have witnessed firsthand memories of strangers coming to them, but the memories had belonged to people from before their time period.

Does Christianity accept reincarnation? Some argue the Bible testifies to reincarnation as it is said, John the Baptist was referred to as Elijah (*King James Version*, Mark 6:14-15). Another proof of reincarnation within the Bible people refer to is Jesus who had said, "Verily, verily, I say unto thee, Except a man be born again, he cannot see the kingdom of God" (*King James Version*, John 3:3). People will always argue about the facts unknown to us. The fact remains if you the individual believe in it or not. It is the faith of the believers.

While not all in Judaism accept the concept of reincarnation, "The kabbalists, on the other hand, do believe in reincarnation" (Jacobs). In fact, Kabbalah has so much literature regarding reincarnation that goes as far as to classify reincarnation into three categories.

The truth is again the believers and their individual belief. Whether a religion testifies to it or not is not the issue, for it is what your inner soul believes in. I have come across various topics testifying the memories of the past are completely the effects of a demon or evil.

I reject them completely, for I believe the love for my Lord, my Creator and my Lord's love for me is far greater and more powerful than any evil in existence. If the evil is given this faith, then are you not saying evil is more powerful than my Lord, my Creator? I believe my Lord The Omnipotent and the complete love of The Creator protects all of whom ask, seek, and knock upon The Door of The Omnipotent.

Today, science has come a long way as various scientists have proven reincarnation to be a theory which they believe. Dr. Ian Stevenson had said,

> "Difficulties arise when reported observations seem to conflict with 'facts' that the majority of scientists accept as established and immutable. Scientists tend to reject conflicting observations..... Nevertheless, the history of science shows that new observations and theories can eventually prevail" ("Ian Stevenson").

Remember when traveling to the moon and beyond was believed to be the imagination of the blessed seers and philosophers of the past. They were told what they say is not true, yet today we have proven traveling to the moon and beyond is not a thought or a belief, but a fact. Reincarnation is also a fact which people throughout this world live with. It is an end or continuation of their quest or journey they were born to complete.

Do I believe in reincarnation? Yes, I do. Who am I to reject a belief that has been proven by more people who live with it, than the ones who but cannot disprove it? I believe miracles from the beyond are gifts our Creator bestows upon us as blessings from the beyond.

My personal journey through this sacred path had left me in the dark until I too found the dreams I had witnessed and seen, were lived by citizens of the past. I do not know why I was shown these dreams and why they matched historical figures lived through the pages of the past. I had written in my book, *Spiritual Lighthouse: The Dream Diaries Of Ann Marie Ruby*, I had found myself in the Netherlands. During a flood, I was in a place called a "fisherman village" in Marken. I helped people escape and knew all were safe.

After my dream, I had researched about Marken and the fisherman village. I found out this truth did take place within the Netherlands. Here, I share yet another dream which I had written in my book, *Spiritual Lighthouse: The Dream Diaries Of Ann Marie Ruby*.

My dream:

> There again I saw him, a complete stranger yet I knew my soul belonged only to him. I was running and trying to hold on to him. There he was running with me. I had

feared the worst as I knew we have only one choice and we must walk up on to the Ferris wheel. We tied a scarf on to our hands to not be separated, and if we were to get separated, then we would have this scarf in between us.

I watched him as we asked each other how is this done? Do we have to just jump off this Ferris wheel and we will end up together again, always forever? I tried to listen, but I knew someone was running after me. I knew I must keep our baby safe. I tried to watch over my husband as he was trying to stay awake and asked me if I would remember everything and if he would remember me. I started to cry as I was lost in my thoughts, for I had no clue. Somehow, I will remember, and I will awaken first. Then, I will awaken him after I have but awakened.

The man who was running after me tried to cut us apart. I did not know what happened, but I was crying as I saw my husband jumping down. I had jumped after him from the Ferris wheel and always knew my child was inside my womb. I knew I had landed on my feet and I had to find my husband and my children. All the time, I knew my baby was still within my womb. I walked as one by one, I searched for my family members.

I knew at the end, I had found my husband, but now the only fight was to make him remember our journey from the past. I saw I still had the scarf as I knew he had half of it but wondered why we were separated and how do we unite. I had no clue about the reality of life. I saw people jumping onto and off the Ferris wheel. I saw on the Ferris wheel, there were children and family members who were separated.

This was a strange dream where all my religious beliefs were being questioned. I knew we have not died and come back to retell what is and what is not, but dreams are lessons from the Heavens above. Where miracles happen, anything is possible. I believe all spiritual miracles do happen at the will of The Omnipotent, for The Omnipotent is the only complete miracle. Spiritual miracles are also called spiritual souls. The belief of twin souls and soulmates is accepted widely within different religious, spiritual, and mythological houses.

The body dies, but the soul lives on as the deeds are counted, and we have Heaven and Hell. It is like reincarnation and our souls live on forever. After my dream, I started to do a lot of research as this was not the first dream on reincarnation I have had, but one of many dreams.

The dream meaning of a Ferris wheel actually signifies reincarnation. I had seen my soulmate, who had landed within the Netherlands. I knew I had drifted off to some other place. Today, I walk with the complete memories of a stranger who might have his memories or maybe he does not.

While working on this book, I had a very vivid dream about an individual who I have never met. I did not know of his identity until *The Answer* film PR team had reached out to me, to write an article about their film. The film, however, was about the life of a student not the guru. Yet on this night, I had a visit from a very sacred guru guiding me from the beyond.

My dream:

I was sitting next to a man who was reading my book. He asked me, "Are you calling the body a vehicle?" I said, "Yes."

He said, "That is what I had always thought. The body remains behind but the soul travels forward. This is called ascension."

I understood what he was saying. It is as if the soul travels, leaving behind the old body. The soul then reincarnates with another body if a job is left incomplete on this Earth.

I said, "Yes, that is what I am writing the book about. Basically, you have the physical body. Physical bodies are vehicles which The Creator has created. A person chooses his or her vehicle and takes responsibility of the vehicle."

We spoke about how when there is ascension, there is a separation of the vehicle and the soul. He said, "Always remember the soul is forever. This world has seen through various religious scholars, the ascension of the human souls. Separation of the vehicle and soul was seen by people, as witnesses had seen Christ rise, and the ascension of Mother Mary. Believe in this faith or not, people have testified to this event. Lord Krishna and Hinduism had also spoken about this over and over again."

We spoke about how sometimes this is very vivid. Children see it more as they are the most innocent. At times, people see the dead walking around where they had died.

When people go to sleep, it is actually similar to death. Your body remains here, yet your soul travels and returns to the body, as you awaken from sleep. Some people have said as people go to sleep, they travel time and see their loved ones. They come back as they awaken next dawn.

Death is very similar to this situation. You fall asleep. You do not feel your body or any pain, yet your soul seems complete. If you completed your job, your soul goes home. If you have not, then your soul goes back to Earth.

He said, "I have written about this. You can quote me in your book." I asked, "And you are?" He said, "Paramhansa Yogananda."

I looked at him and said, "It is nice to meet you." He said, "Include entry and exit. I have researched on it, so include the body, soul, and ascension. Never is there a death for the soul. The body remains but the soul travels."

So, there should be no fear for the humans of death. Death is just a journey. All people should remember dying people do not feel their death.

The dying just go to sleep. It is the living who feel the pain. When the vehicle and soul separate, you leave the feelings unless you have unfinished jobs left behind.

He explained, "Maya, or illusion, is the door. That is where you will find a lot of answers. Everybody needs to remember there is no fear. Like you wrote, there is no fear. If you want to experience death, every night people experience it when they go to sleep. In the morning, you do not feel rested because your soul was separated from your body and returns to it. The dead actually feel rested and leave their bodies as they go forward with their souls."

He further explained, "When you die, you have an urge to go to the beyond. You just want to run that way. There is an excitement to go toward that light. There is a pull. I cannot explain it to you. Walking toward the light, you forget your love of life and just want to go. Sometimes, people look back and have sadness that they left their family behind. They go through reincarnation. Others have an amazing feeling and run toward the door. What an amazing feeling it is to move on. Some of us, however, are able to communicate with others from the beyond."

After seeing this dream, I went to my Instagram account, and was shocked to see in front of me was a post by *The Answer* film recently of a quote by Paramhansa Yogananda. He had said,

"Don't depend on death to liberate you from your imperfections. You are exactly the same after death as you were before. Nothing changes; you only give up the body. If you are a thief or a liar or a cheater before death, you don't become an angel merely by dying. If such were possible, then let us all go and jump in the ocean now and become angels at once! Whatever you have made of yourself thus far, so will you be hereafter. And when you reincarnate, you will bring that same nature with you. To change, you have to make the effort. This world is the place to do it (answermovie)."

As we enter the tunnel of light after death, there are many doors we travel through. I guess if you have finished your job on Earth, you move on to the judgment court. If your job is unfinished, maybe then you either enter through the reincarnation door or the lost and stranded door. Like yogis, mystics, and religious scholars, scientists too have explored the concept of reincarnation.

Scientists such as Dr. Jim B. Tucker continue the work Dr. Ian Stevenson had begun. Dr. Jim B. Tucker has written several books, and while there are scientists who may not be willing to accept reincarnation, no one can prove its nonexistence. Dr. Jim B. Tucker's research focuses on children and their experiences which he links to reincarnation.

Regarding these experiences, Dr. Jim B. Tucker wrote,

> "Though this may seem ludicrous from a materialistic standpoint, the situation gets much more interesting when we take the findings from quantum physicists into account. If the physical

universe grows out of consciousness, there is no reason to think that a person's individual consciousness ends when the physical brain dies. It may continue after death and return in a future life" (Tucker 194).

I want all of you to have faith within your dreams. Never give up your faith, but accept the others as friends who walk upon the same path of life with a different view. As I had said in my book, *Spiritual Lighthouse: The Dream Diaries Of Ann Marie Ruby*, "Perception is but the perspective of the personal mind."

Let us not divide amongst each other but with respect and dignity, grow with knowledge. Blind faith is not what we are all searching for, but the complete faith within a soul. May all humans find complete faith within their inner soul as all walk in union, from different houses of faith, as the one creation of The One Creator.

Edgar Cayce was a psychic, also called the Sleeping Prophet. He had countless experiences walking within the tunnel of light and brought back messages he recalled to all humans. One of the topics he himself was surprised to have learned about is reincarnation.

"The concept of reincarnation shocked and challenged Edgar Cayce and his family [...] Reincarnation was not part of their reality" ("The Reading's Approach"). Reincarnation, however, is the blessed belief of millions of humans walking throughout this Earth.

"Ultimately, the Cayce's began to accept the ideas, though not as 'reincarnation.' Edgar Cayce preferred to call it, 'The Continuity of Life.'" ("The Reading's Approach"). Whether you call it reincarnation, transmigration, metamorphosis, or like Edgar Cayce, "The Continuity of Life," the past, present, and future unite through this belief as they seek each other.

Life is a blessing as in life, we are able to seek answers. May peace and blessings be with all souls who seek an answer to their unanswered questions. Today, we have the religious and scientific scholars walking with us to decode the mysteries of life.

Prayers are my complete solace for my inner soul. Within prayers, I find my freedom from all divisions of society. I find peace in the knowledge we the humans can unite with the newly found scientific evidence aside from the religious beliefs.

Religious and scientific scholars all have come to an agreement on the entry and exit of life where we are all here for a short time. Let us in union pray for those of us whom believe in reincarnation. Let us also pray for those of us whom do not believe in reincarnation, yet we believe in each other.

For this chapter, I have written a prayer for all whom need a helping hand.

MY REINCARNATION

My Lord, my Creator,

From dawn through dusk, until dawn,

This life is but complete.

Within each blessed day,

We but live completely until the new day.

From the first sunrise till the blessed darkness,

We but learn the lessons of life.

My Lord, my Creator,

Blessed be the dawn,

Blessed be the day,

Blessed be the afternoon,

Blessed be the dusk,

And blessed be the nightfall.

For after this day but ends,

It is then I, Your creation, but awaken,

To a bright new day,

With another day filled with hope,

With another chance yet

To repent, redeem, and awaken

Sin free, pure, and clean.

Blessed be my Lord but is The Merciful.

Blessed be the night before the dawn,

As my Lord but announces my resurrection,

MY REINCARNATION.

After life ends and the sacred soul asks The Merciful Lord for one more chance, it is then our Lord answers our prayers. It is then some of the travelers instead of completing the journey back home through the tunnel, return through another door. Reincarnation is a blessed path for all whom but believe.

The answer here is hidden within the questions. Do I believe? I do. I believe within the honor and faith of all humans. As a dream psychic, I have traveled through many dreams of reincarnation. It is not possible to list them within one book.

As I have traveled through the tunnel of light, there were doors for birth and for death. Our journey from Heaven to Earth and back is through the same tunnel of light. If there is a miracle beyond miracles and wonder that is not known to us, I personally believe it is the tunnel of light.

Scientists have done so much research on this tunnel of light or the NDE tunnel. What happens in the tunnel, where people go, and how they come back is similar to what happens within an individual's dream. The content of the dream is only known to the individual travelers.

Whether you believe the other person's testimony or not is your choice. Modern technology has united travelers throughout this world who have retold their experiences with reincarnation. Movies, television series, and news networks all have reported these stories.

You the individual have your own belief system. I only ask you to let the others have their own systems too. How does one individual reject the belief of millions throughout this Earth?

If you believe in science, the NDE tunnel, and any religious group, you will see this tunnel had been spoken of throughout time. I believe in this tunnel. I believe in birth, death, reincarnation, and definitely the pure and complete true soulmates who search for each other throughout eternity.

CHAPTER FOUR

TRUE SOULMATES: THE TWIN FLAMES

"Soul to soul, mind to mind, body to body, you call upon one another throughout eternity. The separation had given you your identity, yet in union you are complete."

-Ann Marie Ruby

As the sun sets and bids her farewell, Mount Rainier reflects within the glow and is an amazing miracle for all who witness. I know I must light the candles of prayers for dusk. I love watching the sunsets within the vast skies as a reminder dawn too shall arrive after a dark night ahead of us.

As I was watching Mount Rainier hide behind the dark nights, I saw two geese within my pond take shelter within each other. The morning glories had closed up within each other and had gone to sleep for the night. On this day, I too wanted to crawl in front of the warm fireplace, under a blanket, within his arms. I wanted to hold on to him, wake up with him, and be with him throughout eternity. Today, my heart cried for my twin flame, asking him within my prayers to find me.

Throughout time and tide, through the doors of reincarnation, birth, or death, true soulmates, the twin flames travel within the tunnel of light for one another. Reincarnation had brought me to the door of soulmates, twin flames, and even soul families. Throughout time, the mystics, scientific scholars, and religious scholars have tried to guide us. I hold on to them like a walking cane, yet I must walk on my own feet. The footprints laid upon the sands through my journey of life are but mine and mine only.

With help and guidance from all that could give me a helping hand, now I walk upon the path of soulmates and twin flames. Soul to soul, mind to mind, and body to body, I only await you and your arrival. This is what I the spiritually awakened feel like. I know philosophers have compared love to deep meditation. Love comes from God The Creator, for we are all the beloved creation of The One Creator.

When we find true love within our mind, body, and soul, it is then life awakens with miracles. This love could be different for each individual soul. The concept of soulmates or twin flames has been an issue we the seekers have sought throughout eternity. For me, the love for my Creator is an example of my faith within all miracles. I believe in soulmates, twin flames, and soul families.

When life gives only disappointment and resentment, then we say if only we had someone who knew how we feel. For me personally, I seek only him. As a dream psychic, I know he is out there, yet I always wonder if he knows of me. If only he was here, I know I would be complete. I know we must awaken individually and complete our inner self before we can awaken any other soul.

Soulmates are individuals who sometimes end up in marriages and can break in divorces. A soulmate can be a family member. A soulmate can be a friend as friends are called mates. Friendships, however, can break. Twin flames do not break but become complete. Twin flames are always created for one another. Half and half make one. Twin flames can survive individually but are complete when they are united.

Soulmates that end up in a marriage and know they were made for one another, that they complete each other, are the twin flames united. Always look for the complete union which is found within the true soulmates who are twin flames. If your marriage or your union breaks, then he or she was not your twin flame.

We try to give life a chance and try to adjust, but sometimes things go wrong. Somewhere during the travels of life, we had gotten lost. In death, we walk through the tunnel of light. I feel like even in life, we walk through an invisible tunnel, and at times we take the wrong turn. Upon my door came a question, why could a married couple not divorce because it goes against their religious belief?

Technology has brought within our living rooms romantic movies made from different cultures throughout time. Yet technology has also brought upon us the beaten and bruised faces of women. They have tried to stay within their forced marriages, arranged by their families.

Religion and culture here have become obstacles for these women. Do the women stay in these marriages to save the honor of their families? Or, do they try to walk out of this nightmare to save their lives and the lives of the children that have come from these forced marriages?

Through my research, I have landed upon different religious beliefs. One such belief is there should be no divorce because God The Creator had chosen our life partners for us. This belief did not settle well within my inner soul. Too often, I watch bruised and beaten women take shelter with their children in safe houses, trying to flee being abused or killed by their spouses.

How could a religion force these women to stay in these marriages? People use these incidents to conclude there are no true soulmates, but that all marriages are made in Heaven by The Creator. I disagree as we are neither The

Judge, nor should we conclude the destiny. Within life, mistakes are made and at times, we trust the wrong person.

Then again, some cultures force women into marriages without their consent. We must act according to the individual situation. A doctor cannot prescribe medicine without taking a look at the patient. Then, how do we the people judge an individual without walking within his or her shoes? If you are beaten up and are being abused by your spouse, then walk out and believe in hope. Believe in your twin flame and know your true soulmate awaits your arrival, if not in this life, then in another.

I was told that God created sinners to be sinful and created marriages, so humans blame God for their sins and these marriages. By saying God created the sinners or these marriages, you are judging The Creator. We all have free will and when we choose to sin, it is a path we are taking. We commit sins and we drown all around us within these sinful oceans by forcing our views upon them.

If a religion asks you to blindly do something that is a direct threat to your personal well-being and the lives of your children, then how can you not divorce and walk out? Religion is there to guide you to peace and harmony, not to force you into being a victim of abuse. If this compulsion is what prevents you from uniting with your twin flame, then I believe this is the wrong path.

A person should be free to live in peace and find love and honor. Any religion that says The Creator made marriages in Heaven, so one should try to work with the marriage he or she is in, is right and wrong. It is right because we must work for each other, not against each other. It is wrong because The Creator has given all of us the free will from birth to learn to walk with our own feet.

I have seen in various dreams, I end up at a four-way intersection where I feel lost and stranded. It is then, I know I personally had taken the wrong turn. In other dreams, The Holy Archangels had tried to guide me out of a cave I felt stuck inside. When I have to get back on the right track, it is then my Lord guides me as I have upon my lips the prayers, which I call songs, for my Lord.

Confusion about soulmates and twin flames is created by us the humans as sins are committed actions taken on Earth by the humans. Sometimes, these sins are direct effects of the human forces known as the societal, familial, or peer pressure. God created true soulmates, the twin flames, for one another.

We the humans, however, have tried to separate them by force. Believe in it or not, at least give a chance to this sacred bond. If a person walks into a marriage by his or herself and lives to regret it, then it is his or her own sin. When a society pushes him or her into this sin, it is then a group sin that has poisoned all the oceans of this world.

How did I come to this conclusion? Through my blessed dreams, I have seen the poisonous rivers flood this Earth through individual sins that have become group sins. These days, people even make a joke about how many The Creator could take into Hell as all are but sinning. I ask you the individual, why are you part of the "all," not an individual?

You came upon this Earth alone and you shall leave this Earth alone. Try to find your other half, God has created for you. Everyone has the right to at least try and find his or her twin flame. Give life a chance and never, ever lose hope for any given views. Always remember, you have a direct connection to your Lord, your Creator.

All the other marriages where we try to adjust, are also fine as then sometimes we choose our soul families rather than true soulmates. Please remember, no human voice has the right to ask you to stay in a relationship where your life is at risk and tell you it is The Lord, The Creator's will. It is not. It is the will of those whom force you to be in this relationship.

From the beginning of time, religions have taught us about soulmates and twin flames. Science also has tapped into this system of the unknown mystery where we have various views on this topic. Today, we even have astrologers trying to give advice on how to find your true soulmate.

A soulmate is a partner who stands by you or to whom you have devoted your soul. Your twin flame is always your soulmate and it is when you meet, you are complete. Twin flames are separated from Heavens above and as halves, they find an identity on their own. It is the flame of the other half that burns your inner soul to this complete union of one whole.

Hinduism, the oldest religion around, has acknowledged the aspects of twin flames and soulmates. Within Hinduism, twin flames are counterpart energies. One is the masculine and the other is the feminine. The Father God Shiva is the masculine energy, and Mother Goddess Shakti is the feminine energy.

Shiva-Shakti is recognized as the Father and Mother Gods who in union are twin flames. In union, they are the Ardhanarishvara, or union of the male and female aspects of God. According to one of the Hindu texts, the Upanishads, there is a description of how different creations came to be.

> "In the beginning this was Self alone, in the shape of a person (purusha) [...] But he felt no delight. Therefore a man who is lonely feels no delight. He wished for a second. He was so large as man and wife together. He then made this his Self to fall in two (pat), and thence arose husband (pati) and wife (patnî). Therefore Yâgñavalkya said: 'We two are thus (each of us) like half a shell.' Therefore the void which was there, is filled by the wife. He embraced her, and men were born" (Müller 85-86).

The text continues to explain how the man and woman transformed into animals. Both humans and animals were born, and multiplied. According to the Genesis,

"God created man in his own image, in the image of God created he him; male and female created he them. And God blessed them, and God said unto them, Be fruitful, and multiply, and replenish the earth, and subdue it [...]" (*King James Version*, Genesis 1:27-28).

Later in the Genesis, we see how God created Eve from Adam for Adam,

"And the rib, which the Lord God had taken from man, made he a woman, and brought her unto the man. And Adam said, This is now bone of my bones, and flesh of my flesh: she shall be called Woman, because she was taken out of Man. Therefore shall a man leave his father and his mother, and shall cleave unto his wife: and they shall be one flesh" (*King James Version*, Genesis 2:23-24).

Religions have given their proofs to this miraculous aspect we the humans believe and hold on to. We shall find our true love on this Earth within positive vibes. Remember to hold on to the positive vibes and send positive vibes all around to fill this one Earth with positivity.

The ancient Greeks had a similar concept of twin flames as described in Plato's *Symposium*, "The sexes were not two as they are now, but originally three in number; there was man, woman, and the union of the two." When this creation threatened the gods, Zeus decided to split them with Apollo's help, so now "Each of us when separated, having one side only, like a flat fish, is but the indenture of a man, and he is always looking for his other half" (Plato).

In Judaism, the term bashert refers to "a person's soulmate, especially when considered as an ideal or predestined marriage partner" ("Bashert, n1"). The Talmud and Zohar expand further upon the concept of soulmates and the concept of being destined to be with one's twin flame. Islam also expands on the notion of twin flames in al Nisaa, or The Woman chapter, in the Qur'an,

> "O ye folk! fear your Lord, who created you from one soul, and created therefrom its mate, and diffused from them twain many men and women. And fear God, in whose name ye beg of one another, and the wombs; verily, God over you doth watch" (Palmer).

With all of these religious proofs, it is for the individual to believe or not. Personal perceptions are just that, personal. I ask all of you not to give up on yourself or your beloved other half as life in itself is a complete miracle and where there is love, there is only victory.

I asked myself did I believe in love and eternally ever after, or not? I believe in love and honor, and I believe in my Creator. So, I let my destiny be guided by my Lord, my Creator. Personally, I have been guided by my dreams where I had come upon this aspect of soulmates and twin flames.

Here is a dream from my book, *Spiritual Lighthouse: The Dream Diaries Of Ann Marie Ruby.*

My dream:

In front of me, there was a beautiful cottage with a front porch that was beautifully decorated. There were white rocking chairs with blue cushions, and huge wicker baskets hanging as they were filled with colorful flowers. I stood there and smelled the flowers for a long time until I saw the front door was ajar and all the windows were open. Ceiling fans were making their presence known as they were dancing with the white sheer curtains blowing in the air.

The house looked like a very old stone cottage with all the touches of modern amenities blanketed by the olden charm. There was a huge grandfather clock singing his tune in the corner. The kitchen looked like it was very well used. There was a smell of fresh baked bread. A fruit basket filled with fresh fruits and vegetables was lying around the kitchen.

The living room had all blue and white furniture and the same theme went all over the house. I saw the evidence of love, laughter, and life all around the house. Strange, I felt right at home as if I just entered the pure bliss of Heaven. It was a small, charming cottage right out of a painter's canvas, yet I could feel, smell, and hold on to the warmth and serenity that was within this house.

I just wanted to be there and never leave the house. The strangest thing was that I did not even know where I was or who owned the house, how I had appeared there, but just had this feeling of serenity and peace all over my soul.

I walked from one room to another room as I heard the sounds coming from one of the rooms. I walked into a room where men were in meditation. I never felt like a stranger walking in a stranger's home and this feeling shocked me even more. In this room, I saw men deep in meditation as all the open windows brought a beautiful and serene breeze throughout the house.

I just wanted to see their meditation. I never wanted to leave this house as I read on top of this room, a sign that glowed in the air. The sign read, "The Holy Archangels."

I froze in spot as I knew why the house felt so peaceful. I must say I had such a big relief within my soul that I wanted to cry and shout, "Yes! I made it to Heaven!" I was enjoying my new-found peace of making it to Heaven as I saw a young man, who was wearing all white, just showered, so clean, and pure looking. He came toward me as he said, "Hi! I am Michael, Archangel Michael."

I was speechless for a while as I had told him, "Why am I here? I am just, Ann Marie Ruby." He laughed and gave me a hug. He said, "Yes, I know." We had talked for a while. I wish I had remembered, but I don't know what I talked with him about. I knew I had felt right at home and this was family.

Then, I walked into another room where it said, "The Holy Archangel Gabriel." As I saw him, he also smiled and walked with me through the house as I had talked with him for a long time. The house had in big capital letters written all over, "THE HOUSE OF THE ARCHANGELS."

I asked everyone why I was there. How had I been so lucky to be in this holy house? I knew there must be a message in here for me somehow and somewhere.

I was told by The Archangels not to give up and always know, "Where there is no hope, there is but one," as The Omnipotent always watches over. I wanted to ask what have I given up on? Life is hard. At all times, I am fighting the criticism of humans more on top of all other obstacles life brings upon our plates. One thing I always carry within my soul is faith.

I walked into another room. This room I know I have been to so many times. I felt like I knew every part of this room. Somehow, my whole life was in front of me. I saw my clothes were laid in the closet neatly with another person's clothing. I saw my pictures were hanging on the wall with another man in the same frame.

I saw The Archangels were watching over me as I had walked into the room. There was a huge wall with murals and art work all over it. The murals were also my pictures, hand drawn by a talented artist who had turned my picture into a beautiful art. The wall had my name written on it, all in capital letters. Next to my name in capital letters, it said, "SOULMATE FOREVER AND EVER." There was another name next to my name and I watched the two names come close to each other.

The wall had magical letters appear as it read, "Forever and ever, soul to soul, mind to mind, body to body, we are but one." The two names were in a heart shape and it read, "Soul to soul, forever yours." I do remember the name, but for personal reasons, I will not disclose his name. I did not know any one personally by that name and wondered why my Lord was showing me this.

As I wondered why I was being shown this dream, The Archangels replied, "Please do not give up on hope for hope blooms around the corner. As all is but lost, he is still out there, and he remains pure as you are." They told me life is complicated and when all seem lost and we find no reason to go on, we must remember The Lord has a reason for each soul. I told them I have given my soul to my Lord. They told me they knew, yet there is a human walking this Earth to whom I belong as he belongs to me too. I told them I don't believe in belonging, but just being.

They replied when he shows up, I will understand what they mean. They repeated, "You two shall be one and you will realize as he too will realize you two belong to each other." They asked me not to forget his name. I thought how could I forget his name as it is inscribed within my soul. I worried though that I will never approach any man in my life as I live a very sacred life. I am not sin free and never claim to be, but I have always tried to avoid sins if I could. I cried as I saw then in the same room, he appeared in front of me as he too touched the wall and read my name.

He asked me, "Are we dreaming again or is this reality?" I did not know the answer, but I ran toward him as I hugged him and cried for a long time. I asked him, "How do I find you? Where do I find you?" We held on to each other as I do not remember the replies to my questions.

The whole night, I prayed with The Archangels as my soulmate and I prayed all night for guidance. I woke up with his name on my lips, and I also knew I would not disclose his name to another soul. I had been praying the whole night and had awakened with a prayer within my lips. I wrote the prayers we were reciting. Strange thing was yes, I do remember some of the prayers as if they just came to me.

In my book, *Spiritual Lighthouse: The Dream Diaries Of Ann Marie Ruby*, I had mentioned a few dreams about my twin flame. In one dream, I had seen my twin flame sleeping on top of the water where I tried to awaken him. I shall now talk about yet another dream in which he had told me where he lives.

My dream:

It was a dark night. The wind was touching me and felt like it was piercing my skin. I felt cold and somehow, my feet also

ANN MARIE RUBY

felt wet. There was light pouring in from
above as I knew I had tried to get out of this
place for a long time.

I remembered I had tried to go
somewhere, but I landed in this well.
Someone was sleeping near the well, by the
opening. I kept calling for him. I knew his
name and I asked him to wake up and give
me his hands as I could not do this alone
anymore.

There on top of the well opening, he
was standing. He said he was there and not to
worry. I watched him and saw he was making
a ladder out of rope. I asked him if he was
awake yet. Then, I saw a ladder come into the
well as he said climb out of it. He gave me his
hand and he held on to my hand. I climbed
out of the well and found myself on a green
landing within his arms.

I knew he was my soulmate, my twin
flame and I cried as I asked him why he had
taken so long. He said he had the memories,

but he was scared to say them out loud. He knew he must awaken, but as his dreams had broken, he would forget. I asked him where he was. He said the land of William, the land of orange.

I had awakened to yet another morning where I found my friends at my door who saw interlinking dreams. They said they saw William the Silent and that my soulmate was born in that land from a middle-class family. I found out by searching on Google that the land is known to us humans as the Netherlands.

Whether you believe in twin flames and soulmates or not is your individual choice, which I call personal perspective. I, however, have received the miraculous gift, a message that my twin flame lives within the Netherlands. On Google, I found a well-known human who also received a miraculous dream which helps us all to this day. You ask me who he is? I will shortly talk about him.

In my dreams, I have received the message that my twin flame lives in a faraway land where I must find him. Time will guide me to him. All I have in between my search, my twin flame, and myself, are time and my belief always ever strong. Now let us walk through another person's belief and what he had achieved by believing in his dream and making it into reality.

Larry Page, co-founder of Google, had spoken of his journey in founding Google during his Commencement Address at the University of Michigan,

> "You know what it's like to wake up in the middle of the night with a vivid dream? And you know how, if you don't have a pencil and pad by the bed to write it down, it will be completely gone the next morning?

> Well, I had one of those dreams when I was 23. When I suddenly woke up, I was thinking: what if we could download the whole web, and just keep the links and… I grabbed a pen and started writing" (Page).

Today, because of Larry Page, we have Google. Like him, I too wanted to find out more about the land that kept coming to me within my dreams. Dreams are miracles. They appear to guide us throughout our lives. Twin flames are a fact of this life and are miracles from the beyond. When prayers are recited by two souls to be united with each other, I believe it is then our twin flames call upon each other.

I have complete faith in my Lord, my Creator as I the traveler journey through this life. Hard and lonely it may be, but with my faith as my guide, I know at all times I have Angels upon Earth and beyond watching over me. I shall find the courage and faith I need to keep going with the love of my Lord, my Creator.

As for my twin flame, just like my dreams, I shall wait for him to awaken and call upon me. If you ever wonder what if this waiting is eternal, then what? Love is eternal. I love him, all of the humans, and above all, I love my Lord, my Creator. I know where to find him. When life gives me a chance, I will move to the magical land that calls upon me through my dreams.

For you, I now have a prayer from my book, *Spiritual Songs II: Blessings From A Sacred Soul.*

ETERNALLY YOURS, THIS SOULMATE'S HEART BUT BEATS

From mind to mind,

Body to body,

Soul to soul,

My Lord but creates true love.

Within the union of two souls,

My Lord's blessings are but found.

From Heavens above and Earth beneath,

My Lord but creates one for another.

The Angels above and beyond

Rejoice as true soulmates but unite.

My Lord, my Creator,

On this day, grant me but one prayer

As I but ask, seek, and knock upon Your Door.

May my mind, body, and soul,

Eternally belong only to my soulmate.

Throughout eternity,

May my soulmate see, hear, and know

ETERNALLY YOURS,

THIS SOULMATE'S

HEART BUT BEATS.

Life is complete when and where we have one another, our families, and our friends. Soulmates are found amongst family and friends. Remember when twin flames meet, it is then true soulmates unite. In this union, the half and half become one complete.

Does it mean if you have not met your twin flame, you are not complete? I cannot answer for you. I believe within twin flames, the button clicks and becomes complete. The Merciful Lord has gifted us with our true soulmates, our twin flames, throughout eternity, born for one another or created for one another as were Adam and Eve, and Shiva-Shakti.

This blessed truth was embraced by various religious groups throughout eternity. Believe in twin flames, for it is in this blessed union, peace is but found. Remember, twin flames are always soulmates, but soulmates are not always twin flames. Do I believe in twin flames? I do.

Marriages prove soulmates do exist. Sometimes when a marriage breaks and ends in separation, I believe it is then they were not true soulmates, but a soul family. Twin flames, the true soulmates, are two parts of the one and as these souls find each other, it is then the journey through life is complete. This is where I believe in reincarnation, its course, and its destination.

Various religions have taught about twin flames. Science again could not disprove this theory. I prove this theory through my dreams as you the scientific scholars but have proven dreams as a factual process during REM sleep. As dreams do happen, and as so many are living testaments to reincarnation, I take these truths as my proof that yes twin flames do exist. Belief is proven through the love we the twin flames feel for each other.

Why can science not prove the existence of God and of God's miracles like twin flames? My response is what about the universe? What about miracles? Is it not true that God created man, not that man created God?

Therefore, all miracles are just that, miracles from the beyond. Through the doors of birth, death, reincarnation, and through the union of true soulmates, life is but a complete blessing. For this, we must find the door of dreams within the tunnel of light.

CHAPTER FIVE

DREAMS:
THE SACRED
MESSAGES

"When and where there is no hope, like a lighthouse glowing from afar, come the blessed dreams guiding all throughout eternity."

-Ann Marie Ruby

Washington, my home state, gets its share of rainfall, but after the rainfall, we enjoy the blessed amazing sight of rainbows. I am blessed as I get to see the colorful rainbows appear near Mount Rainier. The sight of rainbows always reminds me the pot of gold must be nearby. My pot of gold, or hope, or blessings has always been my sacred dreams.

From birth to death, and reincarnation, through the tunnel of light, twin flames find answers to their profound miracles through the door of dreams. Dawn breaks through always, as we wait for her arrival. The sun glorifies the Earth as we return announcing our arrival.

The sun always stands still where we had left him. Even throughout the dark night, the sun's reflection glows throughout the night skies. My invisible support is always there. Even when I am terrified of the dark, I know I shall have the sun waiting for me with a bright smile as we the inhabitants of Earth return to him.

Like dawn and the glowing sun, my dreams too have been there when and where I was lost and stranded. They appeared like a glimmer of hope, like a glowing lighthouse, within the ocean, the land, or the skies. Wherever I was, they have always found me. My dreams always arrive glowing within my life like a miracle from the beyond, reminding me there is hope.

I call my blessed dreams, blessings from my Lord, my Creator. What are dreams and why should we believe in dreams? This question had arrived upon my door through my inquisitive mind. I found the answer through a powerful voice from the past. Carl Jung, the founder of Jungian psychology, said, "We have forgotten the age-old fact that God speaks chiefly through dreams and visions" (92).

We the humans today have different religions and different houses of worship. Remember so much of these religions came through visions, or dreams. Faith-based religions have blossomed upon us through the windows of dreams. The scientific scholars, religious scholars, and mystical philosophers have all agreed upon the concept of dreams, yet they still do not know why we see dreams. They have to rely on the individual's complete honesty and what he or she remembers after each dream.

According to scientists, we see dreams during our rapid eye movement (REM) sleep. Scientists have done experiments with people and their dreams during REM sleep. They have gathered evidence on brain waves when people dream to prove their theories. The only thing they cannot agree upon is the content of the dreams.

Why we see dreams is something no one can agree upon as I believe dreams are but miracles. If we travel through the Abrahamic and mythological religions, we shall find all of the religious scholars also agreed upon the miracles of dreams. Prophecies from mystics and religious scholars still guide us today as they have left behind their dreams to guide the past, present, and future throughout time. Dreams have guided the Egyptian pharaohs, Abrahamic and mythological religions, and modern-day scientists. The case has been proven throughout history that dreams are real.

I want you to walk into this tunnel of mystery through my personal journey as I explain why dreams are so important. Throughout the journey of my life, I had stopped at different hurdles as I did not know how to proceed forward. It is then my dreams came to me, always guiding from the land of mystical blessings.

When I started a business, it was delayed and obstructed through human errors. I did not know what was going on or how to move forward. It is then I received guidance through the door of dreams.

My dream:

> I was driving through a road trying to follow a car as the car was guiding me. I had stopped abruptly as I saw flags on the road. The car I had trusted to take me to safety was wrong and had gotten into a car accident. The man in the car had wronged and passed away. There were ambulances and I was still far behind him. If I were to follow that man, I too would be involved in the accident.

> I waited at the junction praying for guidance. Archangel Michael was driving his vehicle and told me to follow him. I had taken a sharp U-turn and went through a complete circle. By the time I had returned to the same spot I was to be, I saw all the cars that were involved in the accident were removed.

> I was worried what just happened, as I saw the door of death was in front of me and it had closed as it was not my time yet. I had

more people in my car and all were oblivious to what just happened. Archangel Michael smiled and told me, "Sometimes in life, you just have to wait it out."

After my dream, I decided to wait for a while and let things work out on their own rather than force them to happen. Dreams are guidance from the beyond where there is always a helping hand waiting for us whom have no one on this world to help us or even give an honest opinion as to what we should do.

The difference between prophetic dreams and lucid dreams is very easy to distinguish as within a lucid dream, you the dreamer can control your actions. I personally do not believe in the dreams that I can take control over. If I change the outcome, then I would not be able to see the truth of what should be, but only what my mind is controlling.

When our inner fear takes over and controls us, our mind wanders off as we see a nightmare. Students usually see they are failing their exam which is a common nightmare controlled by our inner fear. You can take control over nightmares and awaken from them.

You alone have traveled upon this path and you know if you were influenced by your inner fear or if you were given a miracle. Pure dreams are blessed miracles from the beyond where prophecies are found. Miracles are given. The future or the past is shown.

I have seen the future and avoided the outcome by following the guidance from my dreams. You may see you are either sick or you are about to get sick. Many times in life, dreams from the beyond were my only guide. I also refer to the adventures I have had of time traveling to another time period in the past that match history as prophetic dreams. If it is an epic dream where I had no clue about the subject, but in reality, it has come to life, I know this then was a prophetic dream.

Sometimes, you see the same dream over and over again. I have seen reoccurring dreams of the Netherlands as I have written within this book and my book, *Spiritual Lighthouse: The Dream Diaries Of Ann Marie Ruby*. I had ignored many of these dreams until I had family members and friends come over and repeat the same dreams.

In my case personally, others have seen interlinking dreams of the Netherlands, Prime Minister Mark Rutte,

William the Silent, and other topics. I realized then there must be some reason for me to have these reoccurring dreams and for others to have interlinking dreams with me. I still do not know the answer, but time will tell.

Did you have a dream because something in your life triggered the dream? Did the dream remind you of something you had forgotten or ignored? Or was the dream a complete miracle as the person in your dream was unknown to you and you found him or her through the door of dreams? Dreams are in my mind the greatest miracles that I have witnessed within my life.

Separate dreams from nightmares. If more than one person has the same dream, pay attention. Give your dream some time and come back to it. If your dream is a guidance, be guided by it. If your dream is a warning, be cautious. Please do write down your dreams and know someone is trying to guide you through the mystical tunnel of light, if only you can remember.

Why do some of us remember our dreams, but some of us do not? This question had come upon my door. I found out for me personally when The Lord so willed for me to remember, I did remember the dreams. Sometimes I have the same dreams over and over again until I do remember and then I know I must pay heed to it.

In the Babylonian Talmud, according to Rabbi Levi, "A man should always wait up to twenty-two years for [the fulfilment of] a good dream" ("Berakhot" 55b). Remember throughout time amongst all of us the humans, The Lord has given prophetic dreams to guide us. Even to this day, followers of the Abrahamic religions look into Joseph's prophetic dreams.

Some people forget their dreams, and why they forget is unknown. I have seen if you awaken from your sleep abruptly, then you tend to forget your dreams. When the alarm clock awakens you, it is then you forget. Sometimes you know you were somewhere and sometimes you will be tired as you were busy, but cannot remember. Try to meditate before you go to sleep and relax your mind, body, and soul to see if that helps and you too shall see what The Lord wills for you to see.

To prove something, you need science. This world uses science. But here, I want you to take a U-turn and listen to Otto Loewi, a very well-known scientist, as to how he received guidance. He had written regarding a series of dreams,

> "In the night of Easter Saturday, 1921, I awoke, turned on the light, and jotted down a few notes on a tiny slip of paper. Then I fell asleep again. It occurred to me at six o'clock in the morning that during the night I had written down something most important, but I was unable to decipher the scrawl [...] During the next night, however, I awoke again, at three o'clock, and I remembered what it was" (33).

Otto Loewi and Sir Henry Hallett Dale are both responsible for finding what we now know as acetylcholine. Acetylcholine is a neurotransmitter that is known to impact memories and our ability to recall our dreams during our REM sleep. Otto Loewi also wrote,

> "A former student of mine [...] reminded me that in 1903 I had already expressed the view [...] This story shows that an idea may sleep for decades in our subconscious mind and afterwards can suddenly return and become active. Furthermore, this story indicates that we should sometimes trust a sudden intuition without too much skepticism" (33-34).

What Otto Loewi had, is what I call a reoccurring dream. Even though the thought had come upon him in the past, he did not remember or make use of the thought until his dreams years later. I have had reoccurring dreams and interlinking dreams, where my family and friends would come over to retell the same exact dreams I had, yet from their own perspective.

If a scientist can find or confirm a scientific theory proven to him in his dreams, then the tunnel of light is the complete truth. All knowledge is gained through this same tunnel. Whether you believe it or not, is an individual choice, but is it not strange when a scientific theory is found within dreams?

I had wandered upon this path for years until some of my dreams had guided me out of obstacles. This scientist's experience proves we forget at times, but we are blessed to be able to revisit these dreams. I believe the tunnel of light has the door of knowledge open to us through the door of dreams.

I personally believe you fall asleep and your soul walks into the parallel world where you gain wisdom, see the past, the future, and receive divine messages. When people say they do not know how it feels after death, maybe it is like a dream where your body sleeps here, yet your soul travels. When you want to wake up, but cannot wake up because of sleep paralysis, is that what happens to the lost souls who cannot move forward?

Through this tunnel, I have received messages from the dead and living as a gift from the beyond when and where there was no other way to communicate with each other. I have seen people come to me for help when they had passed away and wanted their families to know of the incident. I had seen the future as I told my neighbor that Donald J. Trump would win the 2016 U.S. Presidential Election.

I remember telling her to be my witness for Donald J. Trump shall win as it was within my dreams. I had seen him explain to someone in my dream how he had won the election, but was worried about impeachment. There were two people having dinner and President Donald J. Trump was worried about talks of impeachment. I was shocked as to but when did he win? Was the election over? I had told my neighbor about my dreams as she had supported Hillary Clinton. She was upset, but told me she would keep an eye out for this prophecy.

Dreams are miracles and nothing more or less as we all must remember we are being guided from the beyond for a specific reason. Never should we ignore a miracle as then we have nothing to be guided by. The prophets and religious scholars all have guided us from the past. In the present, we have our blessed dreams guiding us. Pay heed to these blessed sightings as they are here to give us a helping hand.

My journey through life has been dedicated to the blessed path of guidance through dreams. I am known as a dream psychic as I see the past, present, and future, always through dreams. I have been guided to the Netherlands and the historical facts of the Netherlands.

Through dreams, I found out about a gentleman I admire like a father who is but the Father of the Fatherland, known to all in the Netherlands as William the Silent. I walked in the past, present, and future to only be guided by and to guide you. I had seen a catastrophic dream as follows.

My dream:

I was going through state after state, land after land, as there were bankruptcies and loss of jobs. There was a different kind of war going on. I was trying to reach some people as I sat down and cried for the humans.

They were fighting each other for no reason but because they were different. Race, color, religion, ethnicity, and gender discrimination had become catastrophic as the world had engaged in World War III. I knew this war had sprung as the leaders of our nations began to separate us, not unite us.

I had walked into a mosque and begged the Imams to teach that all humans are the same. There is only one religion, humanity within humans. I had walked into the Vatican and begged the Pope to do something and talk to all.

I had walked to the world leaders and asked them to help me do something. I asked them to help get the message out that we need to start educating the children and the adults to love each other, not hate. I walked miles after miles. The sky broke open, and I saw a tunnel appear.

I wondered how we the humans have divided amongst each other. The tunnel looked like a whirlwind at times made out of light. All the humans were walking within it and there was no one being left out.

The Angels were guiding all into the tunnel. I asked, "What is going on?" The Angels told me, "People have divided amongst each other, forgetting there is only one entry and one exit from Earth to the Heavens above. The Creator has given you proof of entry and exit within your dreams."

Why do humans divide amongst each other? This tunnel is also known as the ladder shown to others within their dreams. Believe in it and know within the eyes of The Creator, all children are equal, divided by their own committed sins. If you can prevent one person from entering or exiting the tunnel, then prove you are the great power. Believe in the tunnel of light as this tunnel accepts all creation.

As the light shined upon everyone, all
Angels and humans started to recite in union
"Where there is no hope, there is but one."

After waking up, I had written the following
prayer in my prayer book, *Spiritual Songs II:
Blessings From A Sacred Soul*.

THE MERCIFUL

My Lord, my Creator,
Within Your Hands, everything but is,
And it is within Your Hands,
That everything but shall end.
You are The First and You are also The Last.
You are The Alpha.
You are The Omega.
Within Your commands, everything but begins.
Within Your commands, everything but shall end.
Where there is no hope, there is but one.
Where there is no light, there is but one.
You are The First for You are also The Last.
Protect us as we the dead shall be resurrected.
Guide us as we the living must return.
For You are Wisdom.

You are Knowledge.

You are The Giver.

You are The Sustainer.

You are The Preserver.

You are The Protector.

Within Your commands, everything but shall end.

Where there is no hope, there is but one.

Where there is no light, there is but one.

We call upon You for You are

The Merciful, The Merciful,

THE MERCIFUL.

My dream broke and since then, I have written and published my prayer books. I have also written my book, *The World Hate Crisis: Through The Eyes Of A Dream Psychic.* Within this dream, it was very clear that humans were brewing up hate crimes. It is an art that humans were trying to learn and teach all others.

Who am I to say anything to anyone, or change your path and your way? I am just a human being who sheds tears for all of the creation of The One Creator. I have spent my life in peace and harmony because my forefathers had fought for peace and harmony for all the inhabitants of this world.

I ask you all to unite for the future generations. They too ask you through me a dream psychic, to not take away their peace and harmony as we are but dividing amongst each other through hate crimes. For them, I give you this message: let us unite for each other, not against.

Let the future be blessed and let there not be any more wars as these wars were predicted by the past seers. I ask you today to stand up and eradicate all war, injustice, and hate crimes. Eternity is what our Creator has given us throughout all the blessed miracles of existence.

From birth to death and during the journey of life or beyond death, we have the door to miracles. One such miracle is known to all as the door of dreams. Through this blessed door called dreams, sacred messages from the beyond are received. This truth was first seen by religious scholars and then by scientific scholars, as testified by us the humans.

Do I believe in dreams? As a dream psychic, I must say yes, I do believe in dreams. I know religious scholars, and most humans do believe in dreams. This theory has been proven as scientists have tested brain waves and REM sleep.

I believe in dreams and believe this path has been proven to us by the past and present scholars. From birth to death, through the door of reincarnation, as true soulmates but hold hands, they find peace within the mystical dreams, as they know all these are but the complete miracles from the beyond.

CHAPTER SIX

MIRACLES:
THE UNPROVEN

"The first sight of dawn, and the first bud of spring, are but miracles we the humans share, yet do you accept them as miracles from the beyond or as free gifts taken for granted?"

-Ann Marie Ruby

My Douglas fir log cottage within twenty acres of green lands, is like a staged setting within a romantic movie. This is my home, my blessed prayers where I have found peace and serenity. A small cottage, yet it has the harmony and peace my sacred soul seeks within this Earth. The sacred blessings I find within this cottage are my unanswered questions, answered through miracles.

Obstacles find their way within our life from birth to death, through the door of reincarnation, through the struggles of the twin flames. As true soulmates search for one another, guided by their dreams, they end up at the door of miracles within the tunnel of light. The storms of life bid us farewell after they lose their war with the miracles of life.

I always wondered about the door of miracles, as I know after I knock upon the door for a while, the owner shall open the door. Faith keeps all humans upon the path of belief where we the travelers must keep walking for this is a one-way highway. Throughout our life, we the travelers get off track, lose faith, or just get lost. It is then I believe The Lord, The Creator sends miracles upon Earth.

Religious scholars, mystics, and scientific scholars, were all sent to Earth as givers of miracles aside from the miracles from the beyond. Each and every religion is a door to miracles as these religions have brought peace and serenity within millions of humans and have given them a house of worship. Keeping all religions in one house, we have the spiritually awakened humans who believe in humanity and The One Creator before all and any existence.

I have been asked, what is a miracle? How do we know when it is a miracle? When an event is unnatural and cannot be explained through scientific means, it is called a miracle. These events are usually attributed to spiritual scholars, to religions, or any unnatural sources. I personally call them blessed miracles from the beyond.

Miracles have created religions as we the humans have accepted them as nothing but a complete miracle. In the Bible, there is an incident when the disciples of Jesus had gone out to sea.

> "So when they had rowed about five and twenty or thirty furlongs, they see Jesus walking on the sea, and drawing nigh unto the ship: and they were afraid. But he saith unto them, It is I; be not afraid. Then they willingly received him into the ship: and

immediately the ship was at the land whither they went" (*King James Version*, John 6:19-21).

Miracles have been a part of all religions as these examples are also found in the Old Testament such as in the following verse when The Lord said, "Is anything too hard for the LORD" (*King James Version*, Genesis 18:14). These verses teach us miracles are just that, pure miracles. Faith is the complete miracle I believe we the humans but live within. Through the mythological periods to the Abrahamic periods, we have seen miracles as the basis of religion.

When a patient awakens after years of being in a coma, doctors call this a miracle. Patients and researchers of NDEs would agree the experience is a complete miracle. Witness testimonies of NDEs and complete recovery have been recorded throughout time. These testimonies prove miracles of life are but The Creator's complete blessings. Within science, there is no proof of miracles as scientists cannot prove what they cannot recreate. Scientists must be able to repeat an experiment or observe something repeatedly, but a miracle happens once.

Reiki, yoga, and meditation are all a part of this miraculous journey we the humans travel upon. Yesteryears, we had people who could heal just like the doctors of the modern world, yet these people had suffered from criticism as they had confessed their healing abilities. We the humans have called them witches or magicians.

Some had accepted their treatments, but afterward became the critics. Historically, we had seen baseless reasons for the witch burnings. When a man had tried to guide us, we called him a mystic, but when a woman had tried to guide us, we called her a witch.

Throughout time, we have accepted different miracles as gifts and blessings from the unknown. I believe the doctors are our modern-day miracles as they seek the knowledge to heal all of whom suffer from worldly ailments. When we need a pain killer, we seek the medical professionals. Yet when our soul seeks the pain killers, it is then we seek bigger miracles from the beyond.

For me, dreams have been complete miracles. Science has proven we see dreams. Scientists do not know the content of the dreams but agree we do see dreams. For me, this is my scientific proof of miracles. I ask you the scientists, when you proved the existence of dreams, do you not see it is then you had also proven miracles?

In science, if you can test something out and the results are positive, then it becomes a proven fact. I recently had electricity taken to my barn. When I turned on the switch after the installation was complete, my whole barn lit up. I was jumping up and down as my dark barn now had lights which turned on with either the touch of a switch or an auto timer.

The next morning, it was dark and cloudy. The sun was hiding behind the clouds. I thought every morning I take for granted that my Lord, my Creator would switch on the sun to brighten my part of the Earth. At dusk again, my Lord, my Creator would have the moon and stars appear upon our skies. Every day, our Earth rotates on a timer and brings upon our doors dawn or dusk.

The scientists agree turning the switch on brings light upon our houses. So then, we all must agree, there is someone turning on dawn and dusk, or has an auto timer for these miracles to happen. You the scientist through your scientific theory created the switch which turns on the light. Here I say to you the scientist, your creation is a fact because you created it or recreated it. But who created you and recreates every day? The sun appears not once, but every single day. Your scientific theory proves your Creator. You the creator of your scientific theory prove you are the creation and your Creator, The Almighty, is the biggest miracle you cannot touch.

This proves my miracle is my Lord and my Creator's existence. The complete miracle is but my faith. My Lord also has blessed me with dreams where I have seen miracles take place. Within a blessed dream, I was told to go to the doctor. I had visited the doctor and found out I had diabetes which needed to be in control. This is a healing dream where I was being guided to go to the doctor because otherwise my health would be at risk. It was a miracle from the beyond.

Within another dream, I had asked for the hidden healing powers. I had written this dream within my book, *Spiritual Lighthouse: The Dream Diaries Of Ann Marie Ruby*.

My dream:

> I was standing in the dark with the stars as my only guide. I watched the moon above shine and glorify this Earth with her

true beauty. I was crying and tears had rolled down my chest as they fell nonstop. I cried as in the dream, I felt lonely and knew I was like an orphan looking for a motherly affection from someone, or somewhere.

My feet were bare, and I felt the Earth touch my skin as the water from the ocean washed my feet. The moon shined as I felt all the raw pain of this Earth flood over my soul. Tears fell to the ground and as they touched the Earth, I started to cry loudly. I wanted to get all the tears out from my system. I cried as I saw there were no humans in sight.

I never thought being alone would make me cry as I love to be alone and meditate and feel God and the presence of God everywhere. I guess I also like being in unfamiliar crowds where I meet up with all different strangers and feel the presence of my Creator everywhere.

After I wept on for what seemed like eternity, a sweet voice echoed in the air. It felt like from beneath the Earth, yet it felt like from above the sky, and from within the ocean. The voice asked, "Why are you crying?"

I replied, "I am lonely, and I feel like an orphan. I have lived a blessed life, always following the peace and serenity, avoiding any kind of sin known to me, yet I still feel there are so many obstacles within life. It is hard and at times I feel like an orphan trying to find my parents or I want to know if there is anyone out there for me."

The voice replied, "But, you know I am always there. I have never left and will always be there. I am in the water. I am in the air. I am in the skies. I am in the light. I am in the Earth. All around you, I am. Never my child, are you alone as you walk above me, upon my chest. Know this, I but am your Mother Earth. I am this Earth and all the mysteries are but hidden within my chest. Within my chest, I, your Mother Earth, have buried all the healing ointment for within me, lie all the secrets of eternity. Within the Cosmo lies the eternal truth of all mysteries, not given to the human mind for it is not within the will of The Creator to reveal this truth for the human minds only have what was given to them by The Creator. The Creator has not only created the humans, The Angels, the animals, the known, and the unknown of this universe, but also all that are above and beyond are but the creation of The One Creator. My child, know the truth. If the human creation is but alive, how is it then the humans think all other creation of The Creator are but not alive? If a human only lives a hundred years, how old do you think I am? Are all humans not born from my chest and buried within my chest? Yes, we are all alive my child. The whole Cosmo is but alive and is watching over all of the creation of The Creator. The truth is I am always here watching over you and never have I left you nor shall I ever leave you."

I asked, "Why do I hurt so much?" The voice said, "For all physical illness, you look no further than this Mother Earth. Within my chest are hidden all the answers to all physical illnesses. Try to go outside and stand upon the Earth bare feet. As you meditate, you shall see the healing powers of the Earth heal you. For all other pain and struggles of life, look no further than the Earth, the Sun, the Moon, the Stars, the Water, the Light, and the Air whom but have all the answers of eternity. With faith, and The Creator's will, all is but found. We are all a single family and when you know of this complete truth, you shall be found by us as we shall be a part of your family too. The miracles of eternity shall be known to you with The Creator's blessings."

I said, "When all is but lost and nothing is but found, there from dust to dust, ashes to ashes, from a clot to human, human to a clot, all is but found for there and then my Lord is but there."

At that time, I repeated this prayer for a while as I heard again, "Life is a miracle waiting to happen each day. Even within the dark, remember the sun comes bursting through the night's sky. All the answers are hidden within this Earth and all is but found for the seeker who but asks, seeks, and knocks."

After I had awakened, I did a lot of research and found out within meditation and yoga, there are healing powers. When meditating upon the ground outside within open air, the healing powers intensify and heal faster. These facts are complete miracles, yet they have been felt throughout time as these are but complete blessings from the beyond. For even more miracles, I had found not just Mother Earth, but a land known as the land of orange which had also come to me within my dreams.

You the Earthly citizens know this land as the Netherlands, which came to me within my dreams from the land of miracles. I had no connection with and had not even known much about this country, but I had seen historical facts about this country within my dreams. When witches were being burned for being different, I saw in my dreams the famous weighing machines of this land. They found justice within a land where they were weighed and given freedom.

I had walked with the founding father of this nation as he had told me he was from the land of orange. Then I had a strange dream, which to this day remains as a big mystery and a big miracle of my life. This dream is from my book, *Spiritual Lighthouse: The Dream Diaries Of Ann Marie Ruby*.

My dream:

My doorbell kept buzzing as I told the buzzer, "Coming! Let me place a leash on my puppy." I rushed and opened my door without looking through the peep hole as I am short and only stand at a height of about five feet and four inches. I can't reach or see through the peep hole. I wanted to change it, but always tomorrow. I am a very small, petite woman, and here as I opened the doors, in front of me I saw standing at over six feet, a complete stranger.

I had strange thoughts go through my mind such as, do not open the door to any strangers, yet I remembered my own quotation, "Strangers are but Angels in disguise."

I said, "Hello. May I help you? Do I know you? Who are you?" He said, "Oh I am Mark, Mark Rutte." I asked, "I never met you?" He said, "No." I asked, "You are a president?"

He said, "Yes, you can call me that. I am a Prime Minister." I said, "Oh you are Tony Blair, Prime Minister Tony Blair?"

He laughed and said, "No. That was a few years ago. I am Mark Rutte and I work for the..." I stopped him and said, "You work for the Queen." He said, "I used to, but now I work for the King. Prime Minister Mark Rutte."

I know we talked for a long time as he had with him a few people. I also was shocked to see where I was. I felt like the scenery was different and I don't recall if I was in my house, a hotel, or somewhere else.

I know it was one of those dreams where you try hard to remember, what else did we talk about? Why would a stranger, a Prime Minister be at my door? He probably won't even remember me, if he had seen me on the road.

Unless you know of the person or people, is it possible to see someone else in your dreams? The people you see in your dreams are usually the people around you. Or, you put the face of someone you know. But here, I have to agree with religious scholars where miracles are just that, miracles, because I had no clue of Mark Rutte or that there is a Prime Minister named Mark Rutte until I had seen this dream.

This dream proves reality around us could not have affected my dreams as an unknown person had come knocking on my door. By giving his name and identity, he made a bridge for me to travel to the land he is the leader of. For more than a thousand nights, I had seen this land calling me from far away. I did not know the identity of this land even after visits of William the Silent and others, until this honorable person had appeared upon my door.

It is a fact that our Creator has created us, but this is not proven by the scientific scholars. Dreams are a fact. The content can never be proven as they remain a mystery to all but the individual. I testify the content of the dream is a pure miracle from the beyond. For me, this dream was nothing but a miracle.

After this dream, my friend had come to visit as she said she had a dream where she saw a history professor came to visit my home. I finally had the courage to look up on the computer "Mark Rutte Prime Minister." There in front of me was the honorable Prime Minister with all the details of a land called the Netherlands. Prime Minister Mark Rutte, a historian, is also a professor as he still teaches to this very date. I have no clue why I had seen this honorable man, but maybe the future shall be my guide, as I believe dreams take time to come to life.

For years, all the details about this land's history had been shown to me. I searched for the events, but I had no name of a land, so I could not find the blessed land. My dreams had started in 2011 and finally in 2016, I realized which land had come to me throughout these years, as I had the leader of this nation knock upon my door as well as the Father of the Fatherland, William the Silent.

Dreams are the biggest miracles we the humans have upon us. They have guided the past, they guide the present, and shall guide the future. If you ever feel lost and tired, and you feel like you are walking through the obstacles of life, please have faith in yourself and your inner power of miracles. Critics of dreams have said, dreams are of things you are surrounded by and knowledge known to you. I ask you then, why I did I have a dream of a person completely unknown to me from a country I was not familiar with? I believe dreams are the biggest miracles where we find the answers to the unanswered questions of life.

Srinivasa Ramanujan, a mathematician, had experienced miracles within his dreams. Despite the fact that he had no formal education in mathematics, he excelled in mathematics. To this day, mathematicians and physicists remember him and we have what is called the Ramanujan theta function which happens to be "the heart of string theory in physics" ("Srinivasa Ramanujan").

During Srinivasa Ramanujan's "short lifetime he produced almost 4000 proofs, identities, conjectures, and equations in pure mathematics" ("Srinivasa Ramanujan"). How was it possible for him to come up with all this that was unknown to him? Srinivasa Ramanujan explained that he would see dreams. He described,

> "While asleep, I had an unusual experience. There was a red screen formed by flowing blood, as it were. I was observing it. Suddenly a hand began to write on the screen. I became all attention. That hand wrote a number of elliptic integrals. They stuck to my mind. As soon as I woke up, I committed them to writing" ("Srinivasa Ramanujan").

Through his dreams, he miraculously received information that would make him one of the greatest mathematicians.

Scientists have not proven the theory of miracles. It is not proven why a miracle happens. Nevertheless, miracles exist just like the first blessings of dawn come upon our life as a miracle from the beyond. Here I want to give you yet another gift from my prayer book, *Spiritual Songs II: Blessings From A Sacred Soul.*

FIRST BLESSINGS
OF DAWN

Dawn peeks through

And spreads the glimmer of hope

Through the open windows
Of all whom but seek.
I accept Your blessings of dawn my Lord
For I know dawn is but
My Lord's first gift of the day
For the awakened and devoted souls.
This day is but the blessed answer
To the seekers of the prayers.
May we the seekers open the doors and windows
Of our mind, body, and soul,
And accept all the blessings of this glorious day.
My Lord, may this day
End the hurdles of the dark night.
May they disappear
Through the first blessings of dawn.
My Lord, may I, Your creation, awaken
Sin free, pure, and clean,
As I accept the sacred blessings of this day.
Blessed be the day.
Blessed be the blessings of my Lord.
Blessed be the
FIRST BLESSINGS
OF DAWN.

Life on this Earth is a sacred blessing, where differences are forsaken through miracles. Where and when there is no hope, like a miracle, hope appears through the blessed hands of the magical healers of this Earth. Miracles appear through the doors of faith and belief. The scientists and religious scholars all have agreed when no explanation is found, then it is a pure miracle. Miracles are just that, a miracle where no explanation is needed or given.

Religions have formed through the faith of miracles. Doctors and scientists perform miracles each and every day as they too witness miracles in front of them. Tomorrow at dawn, as you step outside to take a fresh breath of morning air, do believe there is someone who has turned this dawn on for you. This is the miracle known to all of us as The Lord, The Creator.

Do I believe in miracles? I do. When the reasoning cannot be explained even through science, it is then we call something a miracle. A dead person coming back to life after being pronounced dead by the doctors is a miracle. Receiving messages from the beyond through dreams is a miracle. I believe in miracles as I believe in all humans to be the complete miracle of our Creator.

How can I not believe in miracles? These psychic eyes have seen birth, death, reincarnation, true soulmates, and dreams are all but miracles from the beyond. Yet, I agree as everything begins, everything must also end.

CHAPTER SEVEN

END OF TIME:
THE CONSORT OF LIFE
IS DEATH

"Life sings the sweet tunes of joy and sorrow until she completes her journey, for then she welcomes her consort with a blessed kiss as she sings goodnight."

-Ann Marie Ruby

Dawn peeks through, above Mount Rainier as she reminds me how beautiful and peaceful she looks and feels. The fresh mountain air is what had brought me to this secluded place which I call my haven. Yet today, I watched this very mountain and had to remind myself she is asleep. One day, she will awaken and will be erupting over all that is around her. The mountain is a beautiful sight as she has witnessed so much life around her. Yet it is predicted by scientists, one day she will end all that is around her for Mount Rainier is one of the most dangerous active volcanoes on this Earth. I know all that had begun must also end, as the consort of life is death.

From the beginning of time, we the humans have walked upon the paths of birth, death, reincarnation, true soulmates, dreams, and miracles through the tunnel of light. We the humans enjoy the concert of our Lord's blessings as we know all that had begun must also end. The first sight of dawn announces the birth of a new day upon our life, where hope glows like the glowing sun from within the dark skies.

Hope grows throughout the day as we try to find the meaning of this blessed day. Whatever the day grows to or brings upon us, we know the day but ends as this day leaves, bidding her farewell to us. I have always compared a day to a person's complete life, and I know before life ends, we the travelers have a journey we must complete.

Why were we sent to this Earth? What is the purpose of life? What is the complete journey of a soul? Why do we all have different time periods to live upon this Earth? How could a day lived by one person be compared to a hundred years lived by another person? How is this fair?

After a long period of meditation and devotion on this subject, I wrote a prayer which had given peace to my inner soul. I would like to begin this chapter with this prayer from my book, *Spiritual Songs: Letters From My Chest.*

CONSORT OF LIFE IS DEATH

My Lord, accept my prayer of life.

Life is a circle which must meet her consort.

My Lord, I pray for my life

For it only lasts a day as dawn begins.

At the break of dawn, I pray for love.

Hold my hands my Lord

And take me to the early afternoon.

As the afternoon walks into my life,

I pray for courage.

I walk on my Lord's Path

Holding my Lord's hands as I end up at dusk.

Now my Lord, I pray for honor.

I can barely see my Lord

For dusk is becoming dark.

Hold my hands my Lord as I pray only to You.

My Lord, now I need You the most

For my path leads to dark nightfall.

I need my dignity

For I cannot see, or walk, or hear, or talk

For darkness engulfs all around.

My Lord, I know with Your holding hands,

I shall walk and cross this bridge of my life

For life has given me

Love, courage, honor, and dignity,

But now I give my life her consort for I know

My Lord, the

CONSORT OF LIFE IS

DEATH.

Life begins and also ends, but we the humans do not know our dates of departure. We know we must all enter the tunnel we depart through. What about Mother Earth? She watches all of her children walk and play upon her chest, as she lays them to their final resting place within her chest. She too knows whatever had begun must end, for she too shall fall asleep.

Mother Earth watches all the signs of what has been predicted by religion and science. This prediction is known to you and me as the end of time. Within this chapter, I talk about my personal perspective of the mind, body, and soul, and my journey through this Earth. As always, I look into the religious and scientific perspectives on each subject.

The scientists are worried about the end of time predictions of religions and the past seers. The Earth is showing signs of these predictions and climate control is taking priority within the environmental issues. Many scientists agree we could delay the effects but not prevent the final outcome from happening.

Climate change and its effects are proof for end of time. Rising sea levels and global warming are some of the facts which have world leaders and scientific scholars worried about climate change and end of Earth. It was predicted this would be a reality. The end is confirmed, but we want to delay this as much as possible. Humans are divided as to their views on how the Earth shall come to an end.

Science depends on being able to turn a switch on and off repeatedly to give us results. Human existence, the arrival of humans, or the departure of humans are unknown and cannot be proven. Science cannot prove where we came from as theories differ within different researches.

Science proves through research that humans have come from somewhere, yet they cannot prove this journey completely. Scientists know all about the human vehicle and the human mind. The human soul, however, they cannot touch, so how can science prove or disprove the source of human existence and journey of the human soul?

How can science prove what cannot be seen or touched? According to the Intergovernmental Panel on Climate Change, "Taken as a whole, the range of published evidence indicates that the net damage costs of climate change are likely to be significant and to increase over time" ("Global Climate Change: Effects"). Scientists know the Earth shall come to an end, but they cannot touch time as time is a miracle beyond the human mind.

Pope Francis spoke about where humans came from, in terms of both evolution and creation beliefs in a speech in 2014,

"When we read the account of Creation in Genesis we risk imagining that God was a magician, complete with an all powerful magic wand. But that was not so. He created beings and he let them develop according to the internal laws with which He endowed each one, that they might develop, and reach their fullness."

Pope Francis said, "God is not a demiurge or a magician, but the Creator who gives life to all beings." He also said, "Evolution in nature does not conflict with the notion of Creation, because evolution presupposes the creation of beings who evolve."

Most religions do not agree with the evolution theories. Theories of evolution keep changing as scientists cannot prove what they cannot see, touch, or feel for creation is the complete miracle of God. Creationism is prohibited from being taught in U.S. schools for it goes against the U.S. Constitution's First Amendment which grants freedom of religion. Up to this day, science has not been able to prove creationism.

I take their disagreement or their theories as a complete proof of God The Creator. All know there was something from which we have come down upon Earth. Scientists have proven humans exist as I am a living example and so are you. They have proven people do see dreams, miracles are reality, and humans come from somewhere and after our life spent on Earth, we go somewhere.

With the NDE theories, scientists have proven we enter a tunnel and that is all they know. Through dreams, it is proven that the deceased communicate with the living. Now there are ghost hunters proving the dead can communicate. All of these theories prove the existence of God The Creator controlling all from beyond.

How everything had begun is a sacred blessing only our Creator knows. Why are we here? What is the purpose of life? The unfinished business of the human soul is what we the living and the lost souls all have in common. We journey through life and it seems like our journey continues even after death. We all know Mother Earth too shall fall asleep and all shall end.

Life on this Earth I believe is but a day. If a person lives one hundred years or just one day, your journey through life was completed as you entered and exited this Earth. We were sent here for a purpose and I believe each individual has a different role he or she is partaking on this Earth.

My theory is as the War in Heaven had begun, we had entered the Earth, or were sent to Earth, where we are taking a test for our Lord, our Creator.

My dream:

I had seen all different religious groups of people were walking within a field and were worried. Everyone was trying to find The Teacher, or The Principal as everyone had their final exam papers in their hands. I had again been blessed to be with The Holy Archangels watching this group of people which never ended. I had seen people were searching for the house of Moses. They were searching for the house of Christ. They were searching for the house of Krishna.

People were trying to run and be ahead of all. I started to cry, and tears had fallen from my eyes non-stop for all of the human population. Instead of trying to find peace or work for each other, all were fighting against each other. I cried and tried to tell all to unite. I asked The Holy Archangels who is right and who is wrong, for all have traveled through the tunnel of light to only find peace in Heaven.

What happens now? Who passes and who fails the exams? The Holy Archangels told me they must first unite for each other and learn to love all as God The Creator loves all of the children. How could The Lord, The Creator discriminate against the creation? Are all not but the creation of The One Creator?

I had seen some people were baffled at what was happening as they fell to the ground crying. They never followed any house as they could not decide which house was the right house and which one was the wrong house. I asked what I could do to spread the message of peace.

How do I tell all that the journey through life is a test for you the human? So, walk in peace with each other. I saw differences are only on Earth, but remember we all enter this life and exit this life the same way, through the tunnel of light. I had repeated all night, "the consort of life is death."

All religions are here to guide you the human through your test on Earth. After my dream, I realized the end of time shall be. For the departed, the day he or she dies is the end. Science has proven the Earth shall end, but scientists cannot give a specific time as it is within the knowledge of The Creator.

Life on Earth is a test for you to accept yourself as a creation of The One Creator. I have written my prayers which I call songs to awaken all humans to their own humanity. I believe the purpose of life is to accept oneself and all as the creation of The Lord. As we accept our own self as the creation of The One Creator, our mind, body, and soul unite and become complete.

The realization dwells upon us, the complete journey consists of birth, death, and the lessons of life. I believe our journey through life is different as we are given a fair chance to repent, redeem, and awaken. Some only live a day and some live one hundred years or more because their itineraries for things to do or achieve are different.

Even in a day, you the sacred soul but achieve what some cannot achieve in one hundred years. Life is completely fair even though it may not seem so at times. The day lived is equivalent to one day or one hundred years. The day lived by a soul is blessed by The Lord as the beloved creation returns to The Lord. It matters not why you were here and how, but why you love your Lord. How do you expect to greet The Lord as your life begins after this test ends?

Remember the love of our Creator is immense and has no bounds. Awaken from your inner soul as you accept life as a complete miracle from the beyond. Never fear death for we learn to walk and learn to live through all the obstacles. We were given the blessed repentance and redemption to awaken within love of our Creator.

What happens to you the humans who follow no religion or think you have an immense amount of sins within your mind, body, and soul? Here is another dream from my book, *Spiritual Lighthouse: The Dream Diaries Of Ann Marie Ruby*, to guide you in this situation.

My dream:

> I was walking in the middle of a place, but I could not figure out where I was. I wondered, where was I? I saw all around there was death, and the horror of death filled the air. I saw the dead were being carried to the churches and some to worshipping places of individual faiths to be buried. I knew all around were people of different faiths and I was worried what happens after death.

> I saw now, there was a man who was being taken by The Angels as he had passed away. I saw he was tagged a sinner and for his sins, he was being taken to Hell directly. I saw the man was a complete stranger, yet I could feel his complete feelings. I could feel his fear and his terror as I started to cry for him.

> I started to cry to The Holy Spirit as I bent over and started to pray. I saw in front of

me were The Holy Archangels of Heaven. They said, "Watch." I saw the man was crying as he was a sinner and all throughout his life, he had lived within sin. He was born in an orphanage and never knew what to do about religion. He never followed one religion as all the different religions confused him. He knew he had no basic moral values as he always blamed everything all around him for all things that had gone wrong within his life and for being an orphan.

He had blamed God for not giving him a family or anyone to guide him. So, he never tried to fix anything, but kept a grudge over life. At the end of his life, he wanted to follow a religion or a faith, but did not know which house to enter and how to pray. He had bought a prayer book he had found on the internet for all race, color, and religion. He had recited a prayer within the book that was written by someone who said even if all is but lost, repent.

He was reciting the repentance prayer and had called The Omnipotent to accept his repentance and punish him for his sins. He asked The Omnipotent to accept him as he too is a creation who belonged within no house of faith, yet he is a creation of The One Creator, The Omnipotent. He cried to The Omnipotent as he had asked what his sin was. He only knew what was taught to him. Every one of the existing religions claim they belong in Heaven and all others belong in Hell. So, do all people then go to Hell?

The Archangels had heard him and within his dreams, they had come to visit him. They had told him The Lord accepts the repentance from the soul. The Creator has given all humans on Earth the biggest grace through repentance. When repentance comes from the soul, The Lord but hears. They told him if he has no religion to follow or any guidelines to live by, then follow basic moral values. They coincide with all different religions and messages.

I saw on his chest was a book which had written on it, *Spiritual Songs*. Archangel Michael then asked me, "Have you written the songs yet?"

I asked him, "What? I am confused for as a Christian, we are taught to repent and let all faiths coincide with each other. All religions teach the same message. Why don't we realize and just pray even in normal worldly terms?" Then, Archangel Gabriel had asked, "The songs, have you written them yet?"

I told them I want to write a prayer book for all race, color, and religion, something we the creation could recite even without any religious background, just from each soul for The Creator. I told them my only fear is what about all the critics? What will they say? I don't ever want to be known or criticized. I just want to live my life in peace.

They watched me and said they understood this world is hard, but also within this world, there are some people who need a sister, or a brother to hold their hands even outside of a religious house and say with the purest heart, "Just repent to your Creator from your house." I did say to The Archangels, "Would this not be called a contradiction of faith?"

I then realized no. It would not be a contradiction for if I had something all race, color, and religion could recite in union and individually that had no religious background, but for all creation of The Creator, then it would just be a book.

The Angels had hugged me and said, "Anyone is welcome in the House of The Lord for all are but the creation. No human can stop another human from entering the Doors of Heaven." I asked them, "So, how do we enter Heaven?" They replied, "Repentance, the Bridge to Heaven."

I was blessed to have within my life these blessed dreams. I have now shared them with all of you. Whether you accept them or not, is your choice. I believe whichever path we choose to travel upon this day of our life, we only need to carry with us, the basic moral values where we respect and accept all as the creation of The One Creator. Let us not be The Judge but remember at all times it is we who are the judged.

I have written my prayer books in a series of two and have named them *Spiritual Songs: Letters From My Chest*, and *Spiritual Songs II: Blessings From A Sacred Soul*. Remember my prayers are just words written from my inner soul for all whom are lost and need a friend. We have so much we want to say to our Lord, but our thoughts and feelings get lost. For this, I have placed my thoughts, my teardrops for my Lord and all of my Lord's creation into prayers I call songs.

As I had seen the blessed dreams, I decided I must give something back to all of the humans who are trying to enter the one house of The Creator. I believe this life is but a day and we are all the travelers. Light a candle for all as you the traveler find your destination.

Here, I share a prayer from my book, *Spiritual Songs: Letters From My Chest.*

LIFE ON THIS EARTH IS BUT A DAY

My Lord The Most Merciful,

I seek forgiveness in You from all sins of this day.

May my day be filled with Your mercy.

May I be only on Your Path throughout my day.

May I be an example of Your true devotee.

May my prayers reach Your Door my Lord.

May the mornings be glorified

With Your blessings my Lord.

May the sun shine throughout every household

On this Earth in Your name my Lord.

May all Your creation know of their Lord,

The Omnipotent, before night falls my Lord.

May all of Your children know my Lord,

LIFE ON THIS EARTH IS

BUT A DAY.

All that had begun shall end. The sun is always there as we go around the sun. The scientists, however, have said the sun too shall fall asleep. It is then, we the creation shall be left in the dark. The end of everything shall be. Even

154

science talks about this as we fight climate change, only to extend our one Earth, our sun, and all of this to last even one more day.

Science has different theories regarding the end of time. Some point to global warming and climate change. "Effects that scientists had predicted in the past would result from global climate change are now occurring: loss of sea ice, accelerated sea level rise and longer, more intense heat waves" ("Global Climate Change: Effects").

Others believe climate change is not a problem and do not fear end of Earth. Science has Big Bang and evolution theories for the birth of the world. "Science has outlined four ways that our universe could meet its doom. They're called the Big Freeze, the Big Crunch, the Big Change and the Big Rip" (Becker).

These theories prove all that begins shall end, as believed by different religious scholars. Life on this Earth is but a day, so unite for each other. This Earth too shall fall asleep as we all do at the end of our individual journeys. Mother Earth keeps all of her children safe within her chest even as she falls asleep.

Remember the tunnel of light I have spoken about throughout this book. The tunnel is our entry and exit from and to the beyond. Mother Earth waits and allows all of the creation to enter through this tunnel before she falls asleep. It is then, Mother Earth has done her job. Do not fear how this Earth shall end. Besides science, many have prophesied the end of time. Different religions believe someone will appear on Earth to guide all during this time.

The Abrahamic religions and the mythological religions may differ, but all talk about the end of time. Within Judaism, we shall have the end of days when the Mashiach or Messiah shall come to rule. Within Christianity, we shall have the resurrection when Jesus Christ, Son of God, shall have his Second Coming to rule.

Within Islam, we shall have the Judgment Day before which Jesus Christ, a prophet, shall come on his Second Coming with the Mahdi. Within Hinduism, Kalki, the tenth avatar of Lord Vishnu shall come to rule during Kali Yuga which is the last world stage before we go back to the first world stage.

Where there is faith, all the believers walk upon their respective paths. Each religion has different beliefs and descriptions of how the end of time shall be, but these particular religions agree that there will be someone who will help the believers of each religion. I can say from walking through the scientific, religious, and mystical views, the world will end.

Nostradamus was an astrologer, a physician, and one of the most famous seers of all time. He left behind many predictions which people link to the end of time. Although his quatrains are out of order, many of the quatrains contain similarities to different religions. Within his quatrains, he gives clues as to the one who shall come to rule and guide all. The following are only some of his quatrains that possibly speak of a messiah or savior.

> "Victory of the faith with the sea's name
> Over the heirs of Adaluncatif :
> This stubborn, lamented sect shall be afraid
> Of the two wounded by Aleph & Alif"
> (Century 10, Quatrain 96).

According to Nostradamus, the one to come, or the religion of this individual, shall have something to do with a sea's name.

> "From water's triplicity shall be born

One who shall make Thursday his day of feast :

His fame, praise, reign, & power shall increase,

By land & sea he shall war his way east"

(Century 1, Quatrain 50).

The one to come shall have three water signs. Perhaps this individual is linked to three water zodiac signs—Pisces, Cancer, Scorpio, and celebrates something on Thursdays. Or, maybe this individual is born where there are three rivers.

"Long awaited, he shall never come again

To Europe, but in Asia shall appear,

One who from mighty Hermes does descend,

Of all the eastern kings the most revered"

(Century 10, Quatrain 75).

According to Nostradamus, the one to come shall come from Asia. These are three quatrains out of many that describe an unknown individual. I know every religion can take these quatrains and link the individual described to the messiah, savior, or ruler they wait for.

Who is this individual for whom different religions wait? When will end of time be? Each human is a lonely traveler taking a journey through life. We have each other for guidance and support, yet we must walk with our own feet.

We the humans shall try to keep this Earth safe for our future generations to have the same chance in life just as we did. Guidance they will find throughout our footprints, yet they too must enter and exit by themselves. I realized my mind did not fear how the world will end as I believed in this theory and know all that had begun shall end.

I believe the end of time is also the beginning of the unknown. My blessed dreams have taught me to live a peaceful life where I know even after death, life begins again. Never fear the end but have faith within the unknown and believe in the tunnel of light as a miracle from the beyond. This tunnel is there as a guiding light for all of the creation to have faith.

For all of you, I give another prayer from my book, *Spiritual Songs II: Blessings From A Sacred Soul.*

THROUGHOUT ETERNITY

My Lord is but my saving grace.
My Lord is but my faith throughout eternity.

My Lord is but the only hope I have, I hold,

And I shall belong to throughout eternity.

As the skies turn dark

From the storm brewing above the Earth,

As the Earth cracks beneath our feet,

As the oceans flood all over the lands,

Destroying homes and lives,

Even then I hold on to my faith

As the End of Time but brews

All around the Earth.

My Lord, my Creator,

This mind, body, and soul have been in devotion

For You throughout eternity.

Even when all but had begun, I was in devotion,

And when all but shall end, I, Your devotee,

Will be in complete devotion for

My Lord, my Creator.

Within my Lord is but all of my faith.

Within my Lord, all humans are but one

As we the humans are all but the creation

Of This One Creator.

Oh my Lord, I ask of You on this day,

Even when all that is but ends,

Even when nothing is but left,

Even then, may this devotee's

Eternal love for my Lord, exist

THROUGHOUT

ETERNITY.

We know when and where everything begins, everything must also end. For this, we celebrate the birth of a child. As the same human bids his or her farewell to all on Earth, we also celebrate his or her life lived on Earth. All the scientists and religious scholars agree Mother Earth too shall come to an end.

The complete miracle that allows all of this to happen is the complete Omnipotent and The Omnipotent's miracle tunnel, which I call the tunnel of light. Do I believe everything that begins shall also end? I do. Dawn brings upon us a new day and at sunset, the day bids farewell to us.

I know we the humans enter this Earth through the door of birth and must leave this Earth through the door of death. When this happens, it is the end of world for that individual person, proving the consort of life is death. This world that had taken birth also shall end as all the scholars but believe.

After the long journey, we the travelers should always remember to accept this life from birth to death, through reincarnation, as we unite with our true soulmates. Through the mystical door of dreams, we find all the miracles from beyond. This journey through life must accept her consort also known as death for the end is confirmed and acknowledged as the end of time.

Proof is needed for the doubtful minds. For a mind that believes in birth, death, reincarnation, true soulmates, dreams, and miracles, I do believe. Like all the proofs given to us throughout time, when all but ends and this Earth is no more, it is then what we call, the end of time.

CONCLUSION

ETERNAL TRUTH: THE TUNNEL OF LIGHT

"Ask, seek, and knock, our mind, body, and soul were taught, yet when the unanswered questions of life knock, seek, and ask upon our door, it is then we open the doors to faith."

-Ann Marie Ruby

Dusk appears, warning us that the dark night is approaching ahead. Within this time, we try to light a candle for ourselves and all of whom are in the dark. The Lord had thought about our fear and had lit the moon with love and glory. To accompany the moon within the lonely skies, appear the guiding stars. Like our Creator, we the humans carry a candle within our hands as we take our one-day trip on Earth through the tunnel of light. At the end of our journey, we take this candle and become a guiding light for all of our human brothers and sisters as we exit through the same tunnel of light.

Buried beneath the Earth with all of our secrets, we rest. Awakened with complete faith as our guidance, we the humans enter the tunnel of light, as we seek the unanswered questions of life. Life is a blessing as we have the biggest gift, a candle within our hands throughout the journey of our life, known as faith. When faith is awakened and spiritual awakening takes birth, it is then all of our questions convert to answers.

Through this book, I have only spoken about my journey through my spiritual awakening. As a young child, I was taught when you can pick the fruit with your own hands, why would you want to use a stick and risk not getting the fruit? Religions are there to guide us, but you are the traveler who needs to walk and take the journey. Try to find a direct connection with your Creator, with or without religious affiliation.

I do not want to prove any religious or scientific views for I believe in basic moral values. Life is a book filled with questions, but here we have no answers. Blessed I was as I have received some answers to my own asked questions of life. Throughout this book, I have not tried to prove or disprove anything, but I present to you what I have seen through my eyes and my personal dreams.

With science, religion, and mythology, I have verified the content of my dreams. I have seen the revolving tunnel of light with its many doors. For some, the tunnel becomes the tunnel of entry as people go through the door of birth. For others, the tunnel becomes the tunnel of exit as people go through the door of death. Through the tunnel of light, I have seen the doors of reincarnation, dreams, miracles, and end of time.

In this book, I have shared my personal views on these topics. Remember, no one has the right to place upon you his or her views or ways for you must walk with your own feet. One message I would like to leave behind with all of you is do not discriminate against each other. Remember all humans enter and exit through the same tunnel. God The Creator has the key and allows all without discriminating. So, who are we to discriminate against each other?

Follow your basic moral values and awaken yourself spiritually. All throughout my life, I had asked for guidance from my Creator. I had asked my Lord, "Where are You? How do I find You my Lord, my Creator?" I had written the following prayer after this quest had taken over my inner soul. This prayer is from my book, *Spiritual Songs: Letters From My Chest.*

ASK AND I SHALL FORGIVE

My Lord The Most High,

I the sinner cry up to the sky.

In search of You,

I climb mountains which reach the sky.

I cross oceans after oceans in sigh.

Oh my Lord, my heart filled with guilt as

I have sinned up to the sky.

Oh my Lord, guide me to You,

Take me back on Your Path I cry.

My Lord, I will walk thousands of miles

In search just of You.

Everywhere I lay my eyes in search just for You.

Forgiveness I ask not of You

But to pull me into Your arms.

It is getting dark my Lord,

So I return home with a heavy heart.

Oh my Lord, my house is lighted up

With Your light.

Tears roll as I hear Your loving words,

"ASK AND I SHALL

FORGIVE."

After this prayer, I knew my love for my Lord is the answer to all the questions I have had for my Lord. Another dream of mine came to me when I had the following questions. Which religion is the correct one? Who shall go to Heaven and who shall go to Hell? What will happen after everything ends? That night, I had an unexpected dream.

My dream:

Within my dream, I was waking up
from my sleep as I saw The Holy Archangels
had asked me to go on a walk with them. It was

dawn. All around, it was peaceful and quiet. I saw we were walking to a mountain where there was a huge crowd. I saw people from different religions were gathered within the foothills of the mountain. I had wondered what was going on as I saw people were being divided not by their religion, but by their deeds. Everyone saw his or her respective beloved religion represented on top of the mountain.

The Holy Archangels only stood as they had the same love and care for all of the humans. They did not see different religions or the wrong or right as they only guided all humans toward this mountain. I was amazed at their love and honor for all of the humans, and how we had divided amongst each other, calling oneself the greatest amongst all. It was as if no one cared what was ahead of us, but only who was right and who was wrong. I kept thinking but why are you the human judging?

A ladder appeared from the Heavens above and in front of me there I saw my Lord, The Holy Spirit, standing and watching all as

The Holy Archangels had told me it was not my time yet. I was asked to spread a message to all the humans. If you were born on this Earth, you are a human being judged. You should only worry about your judgment, not become the critic criticizing all the others who too are being judged. Here at The Lord's arena, everyone is equal.

It was an amazing place to be where every single human was equal just being judged on individual grounds or actions, not for who they belong to or what they believe. They were judged for their own actions displayed. I was accompanied by an elderly man along with The Holy Archangels. This elderly man I have seen throughout my life. I always call him Big Papa. He always wears white and when I need him, he has appeared from time to time.

In reality, I do not know who he is, and I have never called anyone Big Papa. One day, I will know who he is as I believe he is there to guide me and all who need him even at the end of time.

I have written the following blessed prayer within *Spiritual Songs II: Blessings From A Sacred Soul.*

LET US THE JUDGED NOT BE THE JUDGE

My Lord, my Creator,

Forgive me the sinner.

Guide me the repenter

For I, Your creation, walk

Amongst the sinners, the pious, and the redeemers.

I walk all day and night trying to find

The Path to my Lord, my Creator.

I find humans who but claim to know all,

For they but claim to be the right

As the others are but all wrong.

From the early days of past to the future unknown,

They have committed themselves

In this fight of knowledge.

How could all be right and all be wrong

If the messages are but different

From mouth to mouth?

Oh my Lord, oh my Creator,

Even though everything is unknown,

Mortality looming around is but guaranteed.

They fight against each other,

Proclaiming to be the giver of all the knowledge.

Is it not then they but commit the biggest sin?

Do they not then become The Judge?

Oh my Lord, my Creator,

May I not be amongst them.

May I not be the divider.

May I not do unto them what but has been done

Unto all, by the dividers of this Earth.

May I be able to unite all

Within one prayer, and within one house,

The house known as humanity.

For I know there is but one Judge.

For there is but one Creator.

For there is but one path,

The Path of entry and exit.

Let us the creation unite as humans with humanity.

Let us not commit the gravest sin.

Let us but not judge the other.

LET US THE JUDGED

NOT BE THE JUDGE.

Is it not that most of us the humans were born into our house of worshipping? Then, we should be judged by the way we live our lives, not by which house we entered at birth on this Earth. Amongst the different houses we have law abiding citizens and unlawful citizens. This neighborhood I call Earth and the principal, or The Creator, is but The Creator of all humans.

I believe each house of worship is an individual house within a neighborhood where there are different teachers. There are also within this neighborhood, the houses which belong to none yet within the individual belief systems of the individuals. Guided by each house, we live a peaceful life until it is our time to go back to the house of The Creator. Remember to the father, and the mother, all of their children are the same.

The tunnel of light does not say no entry to any religious group. The tunnel has no religious preference. The Creator does not give a VIP pass or identity card separating us the humans. Mortality is within the fate of all humans. So, I ask you if The Creator allowed all to enter and exit this Earth through the same tunnel, then why have we the creation placed cones and stop signs for each other?

All the religious facts that are displayed throughout this book speak of the same aspects, in the same tune, and within the same music. The notes are exactly the same, but sung by different people in different languages and different time periods. It was not possible for them to meet with one another, write up the song, and sing it throughout time. Why? My answer is very simple. There is only one Creator and the messages to the creation were always the same. As we the creation start singing, we change the words mouth to mouth.

We take the concept within our own social behaviors, suited to the land, the culture, and the time period. So, if you cross over the globe from the past to the present to yet even the future through the same tunnel of light, you will find the unanswered questions were always given to us within the answers of The Creator.

We landed upon this Earth with our individual vehicle. We drive our vehicles our way with our own free will. Until we all find our final house, let us drive our Earthly vehicles within the laws of the lands. Remember if you break the law as you drive your vehicle, you are the cause of an accident and for that, you must be accounted. If you shot that bullet from a gun that took a life, it is not your gun's fault. It is your fault for you pulled the trigger.

The knowledge of the beyond was given to us throughout time, through the sacred travelers. These travelers have already driven on the roads we are driving on now. As we travel through the pages of history, we see they are all testifying to the same aspects of life to live with humanity and to hold on to the basic moral values.

Do not do unto others what you will not do unto yourself. Do not take a life. Do not sin. Be in peace and spread peace. Do not divide amongst each other but respect one another. Do abide by the laws of the land. Do not change the laws of the land to suit your own needs, for then you are crossing the basic moral values for your own selfish values.

Religion and science, all are there to guide us upon this journey. Our journey is guaranteed from birth to death through reincarnation, with true soulmates, through dreams and miracles. We end up with the realization that the consort of life is death as end of time must be.

We were given a passport to be on Earth. Whatever knowledge was given to us, was given for our protection. With our birth, we earned the right to be in a certain land and live within the laws of the land.

When we want to enter land beyond our own without a passport, we must acquire the knowledge and guide each other so we know how to cross the bridge with a proper visa. We must earn this seal through the journey of our life. The rule book and knowledge are given throughout time.

Knowledge is given to us for our own existence, so we survive through this journey of life. Is knowledge not given to help you travel from birth to death? From beyond death, we shall get a visa stamped in our passport, so we can travel to our next destination. NDEs prove death is not the end of life. How do you see your body lying behind and you are walking forward?

With our passport, we acquire another vehicle. The spirits, ghosts, blessed humans, and cursed humans are all given a passport and each passport directs us to where we are to be. Some of us become stuck at the terminal and roam around as lost in transit souls. Some of us come back to Earth through the door of reincarnation for the next chapter, either to repent, get a second chance or seek our twin flame. Others may end up in Hell. The rest may end up in Heaven.

You cannot teach the unknown. You can open a school and institution based on the known. You cannot have a school based on the unknown. That is where we have dreams and miracles. Messages come from the unknown through the unknown. You cannot decode how all this happens for it is not within your schools or institutions of the known.

Take the knowledge that was given from the skies, the books of the beyond, or the dreams which are the biggest miracles. Mystics have visions or dreams. Psychics have spiritual visions. But remember, the content of the dream is only known to The Creator and to the individual. We can take the content and live a life peacefully on Earth and beyond.

We need to find peace within ourselves and believe all the answers are being given to us through the door of miracles. Through science, religion, and other sources, we are being guided. Our perspectives and visions may be different, but we should agree to disagree for we live in different houses, different cultures, different countries, and different environments.

Some live in the snowy region. Some live in the mountainous region. Some live near the water. Some live near the forest. Yet, we are all the creation of The One

Creator. We need to accept the differences and agree each society is different and so are our perspectives, our visions, and our views. Remember one path remains the same, the entry and the exit. Everything in between is your free will provided to you by The Creator.

Scientific proof you look for, but do you forget scientists were also created by The Creator? Have I not shown throughout this book that scientific proof also came within dreams through which scientific scholars have said they were able to find solutions for us? Religious proofs are also found within dreams.

Much of the Heavenly books took birth through the dreams of respective religious leaders. No messages on this Earth were received from a human without encountering a miracle. Each individual that had come up with a way out of a situation or a problem was given a solution through a miracle. Many of these miracles were received within dreams.

So, it is true The Creator never left us but kept the tunnel always open. The one-way connection with The Creator is the tunnel of light, or the tunnel of knowledge which is always open to the seeker through meditation, dreams, and spiritual awakening. Whatever you call this tunnel, have faith in this tunnel and remember that we all walk through this tunnel to enter this Earth and leave this Earth. In between, we are given guidance again through the tunnel of light. Accept this truth. Accept yourself and know beyond you, there is a miracle.

Once you know this miracle and have faith in it, the fear that we the humans live with of death disappears. Life is a blessed journey and we are here to guide ourselves and one another. Never let the unknown take you astray. Never fear the unknown, but walk for each other, with each other, and with the guidance of the sacred travelers who have walked before us.

The travelers who are with us or those of whom have left us, are guiding all like angels from above and beyond this Earth. For all of our questions, where and when there is a seeker seeking the answers, there is a star above shining with all the answers guiding from beyond. Until we too become a guiding star, accept all the creation of The One Creator as one family. I believe all humans belong in one house of The Lord.

The fear of losing loved ones disappears for they were blessed to walk through the tunnel of light. They have the knowledge we all seek. The tunnel of light guides us throughout eternity. Know that like them, we shall all walk through this tunnel and meet once again. Until then, be in peace and live in peace.

As I had finished the final draft of this book, today June 2, 2019, I had another dream. I knew this dream was given to be included in this book. For reasons unknown, I had delayed the publication of this book. I guess unknown reasons are the will of The Creator. The dream is as follows.

My dream:

It was dark and the moon was up. I knew I had to find out some secrets that had taken place in Heaven, on Earth, in the past, the present, and maybe the future. I was standing on the river bend where I saw crocodiles line up like a bridge over the river. The moon was glowing and from her glow, I could see the water, and the crocodiles in the river so clearly. I was standing so close to the crocodiles, yet I did not fear them. I saw their tails wagging, similar to what my puppy does when he is happy.

I stood there waiting for something but did not know what. Then, I saw a gondola was coming not through the ocean or the river as you would think, but slowly coming out of a tunnel that appeared through the moon's glow. This tunnel of light came from between the sun and the moon, glowing upon the rivers. As I watched the gondola slowly coming, I realized the tunnel it came through is the tunnel of light.

I watched an old man with a stick do something with his hands. The crocodiles obeyed and they went below the river, letting the gondola land on the water. I saw him and knew he is the keeper of the lighthouse. The tunnel of light here in my dream, I compared to the lighthouse of The Creator, the lighthouse that guides all throughout eternity. It is the same lighthouse that is compared to the tunnel of light. It is the same lighthouse that Earthly scientists call the NDE tunnel.

I knew the keeper takes the departed souls on his gondola and flies back up through the tunnel. Yet, as I spoke with him, he told me he also takes people on this gondola through the dreamland. It is the same tunnel that we the living and the dead travel through. It is the tunnel we travel through in our dreams. When a person is dreaming, it is similar to the body and soul being separated at death.

I spoke with the keeper and we traveled that night through various dreams which I shall not share in this book, but maybe another time. I will only share the knowledge given to me was a blessing as I realized the tunnel which I had been talking about throughout this book was just shown to me by the keeper of the lighthouse. I had called one of my previous books *Spiritual Lighthouse: The Dream Diaries Of Ann Marie Ruby*, as I knew through the lighthouse, we the living are being guided.

I now know the same lighthouse is what we travel through. The keeper hugged me as I felt like I was sitting and talking with a grandfather. He reminded me it was not my time, but he wanted me to take a tour with him through this tunnel.

The keeper blessed me with this miraculous dream. Now like all my dreams, when I awakened, I had to find out the details to see if the keeper and this tunnel existed in reality. Mythologies do speak of him. Virgil wrote in his poem *The Aeneid,*

> "There Charon stands, who rules the dreary coast-
> A sordid god: down from his hoary chin
> A length of beard descends, uncomb'd, unclean;
> His eyes, like hollow furnaces on fire;
> A girdle, foul with grease, binds his obscene attire.
> He spreads his canvas; with his pole he steers;
> The freights of flitting ghosts in his thin
> bottom bears."

The lighthouse keeper who I had seen in my dream is known as the ferryman who takes the dead to the Netherworld. After this dream, I knew the water and the sun had some sort of connection with the miraculous tunnel. Water evaporates and becomes a gas, creating the clouds. After the rain, the sun comes out and we get the miraculous rainbow. All of this is scientific.

The water and the sun create the reflection of light through the moon's glow. The tunnel of light was created somehow through water, moon, sun, and The Creator's invisible force. We can only believe mythologies had some sort of truth. You can believe in the mythological ferry, or the Abrahamic staircase to Heaven, which is also a tunnel, or the scientific NDE tunnel.

The complete truth is given within dreams. This tunnel exists. I believe today I was shown that the tunnel and the keeper of the lighthouse who comes through the tunnel to take all of us for our final journey does exist. We travel through this tunnel as we enter Earth and leave Earth. Do we see Charon, the ferryman? Do we see The Angel of Death from the Abrahamic religions? Do we see the Hindu god of death, Yamaraj? Or do we just go by the scientific evidence, the NDE tunnel?

It matters not for eventually you are the traveler taking the journey as you enter and exit Earth. The final destination is the same as the point of entry. Do not fight with each other or against each other. Unite and unitedly look into each other's faith. There is absolutely nothing wrong in reading the other books that you do not believe in, for you will not lose your identity.

Your name will not change by picking up another book. You will gain knowledge. This knowledge is for your own satisfaction. Gaining knowledge will not change the fact that we all must leave this Earth through the same tunnel, which I call the tunnel of light.

I also refer to this tunnel as the spiritual lighthouse. You can refer to this tunnel as the final exit, the door you must take your final exit through, or the door you entered this Earth through. The time on Earth is to gain knowledge and do right for your own self and for all others. Do not try to prove yourself superior than the other for at the end, we are just the travelers.

Through this tunnel, we had begun our journey and through this tunnel, we end our journey. Yet through the tunnel, life begins again. Mother Earth keeps all her children within her chest, through the end of time. Dawn approaches and ends as she bids us her farewell. At dusk, the journey continues after death. At end of time, Omnipotent, the final chapter begins. This book, however, only covers life on Earth, not the beyond. This blessed prayer, I have written exclusively for this book.

ETERNAL TRUTH
THE TUNNEL OF LIGHT

My Lord, my Creator,

From the first entry of birth,

Till the last exit of death,

I will walk upon Your given path.

Through the doors of reincarnation,

another chance we are given.

Oh my Lord, my Creator,

Blessings from Heavens above

Guide us as we are given,

The sacred dreams.

Through the blessed door,

We the humans, the soul families, the twin flames,

Enter upon Earth.

Through Your door of miracles,

My Lord, my Creator,

Guide us throughout eternity.

Guide us through the obstacles.

Guide us through our journey upon Earth,

For we know the final truth,

With or without any announcement shall come

The end of time.

Oh my Lord, my Creator,

Hold on to us as we,

Ask, seek, and knock upon Your doors

As we enter the

ETERNAL TRUTH

THE TUNNEL OF LIGHT.

We the humans shall all be awakened through the blessed love of The Lord, The Creator. May my blessings be with you. May you all send me your blessings as we unite within the one truth. I call this one eternal truth, the tunnel of light.

Do I believe unanswered questions are just that, unanswered? No, I do not, for how can I? Have I not received answers for the unanswered questions of life through dreams? Through dreams, mystics, religious scholars, and scientific scholars have all proven we enter, exit, and sometimes even reenter through the tunnel of light. Our true soulmates, twin flames, and soul families all walk through this tunnel. The tunnel of light, the one biggest wonder beyond human mind, is a miracle that was given to humans throughout time.

Children have witnessed this miracle. Adults have witnessed this miracle. The past, present, and future shall also witness this miracle. The answers to the unanswered questions of life are simple and have always been there in front of us as the complete truth is, was, and shall always be the *Eternal Truth*: *The Tunnel Of Light*.

ABOUT THE AUTHOR

I have lived the struggles, overcame the obstacles, as I have endured the pain and joy of life as they landed upon my door.

I like to be the unknown face to whom all can relate. I want you to see your face in the mirror when you search for me, not mine. For if it is my face in the mirror, then my friend you see a stranger. The unknown face is there so you see only yourself, your struggles, your achievements as you cross the journey of life. I want to be the face of a white, black, and brown, as well as the love we are always searching eternally for.

If this world would have allowed, I would have distributed all of my books, to you with my own hands as a gift and a message from a friend. I have taken pen to paper to spread peace throughout this Earth. My sacred soul has found peace within herself. May I through my words bring peace and solace within your soul.

You have my name and know I will always be there for anyone who seeks me. My home is Washington State, USA, yet I travel all around the world to find you, the human with humanity. Aside from my books, I love writing openly on my blog. Through this blog journey, I am available to all throughout this world. Come, let us journey together and spread positivity, as I take you on a positive journey through my blog.

For more information about any one of my books, or to read my blog posts, subscribe to my blog on my website, www.annmarieruby.com. Follow me on social media, @AnnahMariahRuby on Twitter, @TheAnnMarieRuby on

Facebook, @ann_marie_ruby on Instagram, and @TheAnnMarieRuby on Pinterest.

BOOKS BY THE AUTHOR

I have published four books of original inspirational quotations:

Spiritual Travelers:
Life's Journey From The Past To The Present
For The Future

Spiritual Messages:
From A Bottle

Spiritual Journey:
Life's Eternal Blessings

Spiritual Inspirations:
Sacred Words Of Wisdom

For all of you whom have requested my complete inspirational quotations, I have my complete ark of inspiration, I but call:

Spiritual Ark:
The Enchanted Journey Of Timeless Quotations

Do you believe in dreams? For within each individual dream, there is a hidden message and a miracle interlinked. Learn the spiritual, scientific, religious, and philosophical aspects of dreams. Walk with me as you travel through forty nights, through the pages of my book:

Spiritual Lighthouse:
The Dream Diaries Of Ann Marie Ruby

When there was no hope, I found hope within these sacred words of prayers, I but call songs. Within this book, I have for you, 100 very sacred prayers:

Spiritual Songs:
Letters From My Chest

Prayers are but the sacred doors to an individual's enlightenment. This book has 123 prayers for all humans with humanity:

Spiritual Songs II:
Blessings From A Sacred Soul

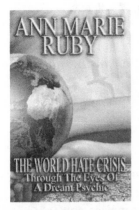

Humans have walked into an age where humanity now is being questioned as hate crimes have reached a catastrophic amount. Let us in union stop this crisis. Pick up my book and see if you too could join me in this fight:

The World Hate Crisis:
Through The Eyes Of A Dream
Psychic

Travel with me through the doors of birth, death, reincarnation, true soulmates, dreams, miracles, end of time, and the:

Eternal Truth:
The Tunnel Of Light

BIBLIOGRAPHY

answermovie. "You can change your life." *Instagram*. 30

May 2019. Web. 2 June 2019. <https://www.

instagram.com/p/ByE8DC7FNnc/>.

"Bashert, n1." *Oxford English Dictionary Online*. Web. 7

Apr. 2019. <https://en.oxforddictionaries.com/

definition/bashert>.

Becker, Adam. "How will the universe end, and could

anything survive." *BBC*. 2 June 2015. Web. 28 Apr.

2019. <http://www.bbc.com/earth/story/20150602-

how-will-the-universe-end>.

"Berakhot." *Sefaria.org*. Web. 27 Apr. 2019.

<https://www.sefaria.org/Berakhot.55b.1?ven=Tractat

e_Berakot_by_A._Cohen,_Cambridge_University_Pr

ess,_1921&lang=en&with=Versions&lang2=en>.

"Dmitri Mendeleev." *Famous Scientists*.

famousscientists.org. 1 Sept. 2014. Web. 26 Apr.

2019. <www.famousscientists.org/dmitri-

mendeleev/>.

"Global Climate Change: Effects." *NASA Global Climate

Change and Global Warming: Vital Signs of the

Planet*. Jet Propulsion Laboratory / National

Aeronautics and Space Administration. Web. 7 Apr.

2019. <http://climate.nasa.gov/effects/>.

"Ian Stevenson." AZQuotes.com. Wind and Fly LTD,

2019. 13 Apr. 2019. <https://www.azquotes.com/

quote/575714>.

Jacobs, Rabbi Louis. "What Judaism Says About

Reincarnation." My Jewish Learning. Web. 7 Apr.

2019. <https://www.myjewishlearning.com/article/

reincarnation-the-transmigration-of-a-jewish-idea/>.

Jung, Carl G. *Man and His Symbols*. London: Picador,

1978.

King James Version. Bible Gateway. Web. 10 Apr. 2019.

<www.biblegateway.com>.

Lyons, Sean. "The Science of Reincarnation." *University of Virginia Magazine.* 2013. Web. 7 Apr. 2019. <http://uvamagazine.org/articles/the_science_of_reinc arnation>.

Müller, Max, trans. *The Upanishads Part II*, (Sacred Books of the East, Vol. 15). Oxford: The Clarendon Press, 1884. *Sacred-Texts.com.* Web. 14 Apr. 2019. <http://www.sacred-texts.com/hin/sbe15/sbe15055.htm #fn_282>.

Nostradamus, Michel. *The Prophecies.* Trans. Richard Sieburth, New York: Penguin Books, 2013.

"Official Launch Event of the International Year of the Periodic Table of Chemical Elements." *UNESCO.* Web. 27 Apr. 2019. <en.unesco.org/events/official-launch-event-international-year-periodic-table-chemical-elements>.

Page, Larry. "Larry Page's University of Michigan Commencement Address." *Google.* 2 May 2009.

Web. 28 Apr. 2019. <http://googlepress.blogspot.

com/2009/05/larry-pages-university-of-

michigan.html>.

Palmer, E.H., trans. *The Qur' ân*, Part I, (Sacred Books of

the East, Vol. 6). Oxford: The Clarendon Press, 1880.

Sacred-Texts.com. Web. 21 Apr. 2019. <http://

www.sacred-texts.com/isl/sbe06/004.htm>.

Plato. *Symposium.* Trans. Benjamin Jowett. *The Internet

Classics Archive.* Web Atomic and Massachusetts

Institute of Technology. Web. 3 May 2019.

<http://classics.mit.edu/Plato/symposium.html>.

Pope Francis. "ADDRESS OF HIS HOLINESS POPE

FRANCIS ON THE OCCASION OF THE

INAUGURATION OF THE BUST IN HONOUR

OF POPE BENEDICT XVI." *Vatican: the Holy

See.* Vatican Website. Liberia Editrice Vaticana, 27

Oct. 2014. Web. 14 Apr. 2019. <http://w2.vatican.

va/content/francesco/en/speeches/2014/october/doc

uments/papa-francesco_ 20141027_plenaria-accademia-scienze.html>.

Smith, Emily Kent and Tania Steere. "Research into 'near-death' experiences reveals awareness may continue even after the brain has shut down." *The Daily Mail.* 6 Oct. 2014. Web. 7 Apr. 2019. <https://www. dailymail.co.uk/health/article-2783030/ Research-near-death-experiences-reveals-awareness-continue-brain-shut-down.html>.

"Srinivasa Ramanujan." *Famous Scientists.* famousscientists.org. 28 Oct. 2015. Web. 3 May 2019 <www.famousscientists.org/srinivasa-ramanujan/>.

Stevenson, Ian. *Twenty Cases Suggestive of Reincarnation.* The University of Virginia Press, 1980.

Strathern, Paul. *Mendeleyev's Dream: The Quest for the Elements.* New York: St. Martin's Press, 2000.

"The Reading's Approach To Philosophy And Reincarnation." *Edgar Cayce's A.R.E.* Web. 28 Apr.

2019. <https://www.edgarcayce.org/the-readings/philosophy-reincarnation/>.

Tucker, Jim B. *Return to Life: Extraordinary Cases of Children Who Remember Past Lives*. New York: St. Martin's Press, 2013.

Virgil. *The Aeneid*. Trans. John Dryden. *The Internet Classics Archive*. Web Atomic and Massachusetts Institute of Technology. Web. 2 June 2019. <http://classics.mit.edu/Virgil/aeneid.6.vi.html>.

Made in the USA
Las Vegas, NV
15 November 2023